Afterlife

Afterlife

A Guided Tour of Heaven and Its Wonders

SECOND EDITION

Emanuel Swedenborg

Selected from the original work *Heaven and Hell*
by Donald L. Rose, Editor

Swedenborg Foundation
West Chester, Pennsylvania

First edition published 2006.
Second edition published 2008; second printing, 2015.

Library of Congress Cataloging-in-Publication Data

Swedenborg, Emanuel, 1688–1772
   Afterlife: a guided tour of heaven and its wonders / Emanuel Swedenborg ;
   abridged and rearranged, Donald L. Rose, editor
   2nd ed. p. cm.
   Abridged and rearranged edition of Heaven and hell.
   ISBN 978-0-87785-325-1 (alk. paper)
   1. Heaven. 2. Hell. 3. Future life. I. Rose, Donald L. II. Title.
   BX8712.H5A35 2008
   236'.24--dc22
   2008032333

Cover art: *Heaven's Gate,* oil painting by Ton Gravelijn (b. 1948 in Waalwijk,
Netherlands). Gravelijn studied at the Royal Art Academy in Den Bosch,
Netherlands, and is known for his symbolic scenes rendered in linocut,
gouache, oil, and watercolor.

Edited by Mary Lou Bertucci
Designed and typeset by Karen Connor

Printed in the United States of America

Swedenborg Foundation
320 North Church Street
West Chester, PA 19380
www.swedenborg.com

Contents

CONTENTS

Part 3: Hell

CONTENTS

INTRODUCTION

The Story of Heaven and Hell

IN THE YEAR 1758, Emanuel Swedenborg brought a manuscript on his experiences in heaven and hell to London where he arranged for a thousand copies to be printed. The book was written in Latin (and the authorship was anonymous), but it soon found its way to various countries and was translated into one language after another. Today, for example, a glossy Japanese version may be purchased in Tokyo and a Russian version in Moscow. Each country where the book is read has its own interesting story, usually involving voluntary translations by individuals who performed their task as a kind of public service.

We focus here on the English version and its introduction in America.

The first readers in England were scholarly folks able to read the Latin original. Some were well-to-do. A case in point was William Cookworthy (1705–1780), the founder of the British porcelain industry. Cookworthy at first was indignant that a book would claim to describe the afterlife, but upon reading it, undertook a personal mission to share this intriguing work with others. He brought it to the attention of a distinguished clergyman, Thomas Hartley

(1709–1784), vicar of Winwick. Hartley also became convinced of the value of the book and collaborated with Cookworthy in translating it into English.

The printing of this first English version cost Hartley and Cookworthy £100 sterling. And so in 1778, twenty years after the printing of the Latin original, English readers had access to *Heaven and Its Wonders and Hell, From Things Heard and Seen*. But how did copies in English reach America?

It happened because a ship's captain owned a copy of *Heaven and Hell* in Latin. During a transatlantic voyage, the captain met a Scottish passenger who was well versed in ancient languages. The captain showed the Scotsman a copy of the rare volume. The year was 1781, and the Scottish passenger's name was James Glen.

Here is an account of what then transpired in the mid-Atlantic:

> As soon as Mr. Glen had read the work, and well considered its contents, he was all astonishment, first, at the nature of the information, which that book conveys; and in the next place, at the goodness of the Divine Providence which had so unexpectedly brought him into such a peculiar situation, that while sailing on the surface of the great deep, of an abyss of waters beneath him, his eyes were opened to behold an abyss of divine truths above and around him. That day Mr. Glen declared to be the happiest day of his life, which thus brought to his view the glories of the heavenly state, and the stupendous realities of the eternal world.[1]

1. Robert Hindmarsh, *Rise and Progress of the New Jerusalem Church in England, America, and Other Parts* (London: 1861), 17.

When Glen reached England, he learned that the book had been translated into English and made plans to introduce it in America. A shipment of books was sent to Bell's Book Store in Philadelphia, where on June 5, 1784, Glen gave the first public lecture promoting Swedenborg's testimony. Among those who attended the lecture was Francis Bailey, a friend and neighbor of Benjamin Franklin. Bailey was a printer by trade, and he became the first person to publish a book by Swedenborg in the United States. Another man at Glen's lecture was John Young, a lawyer destined to become a prominent judge in western Pennsylvania. When Young left Philadelphia, he took with him a supply of books. He befriended an enterprising fellow by the name of John Chapman and was able to provide him with copies of *Heaven and Hell*.

Chapman (who became known as Johnny Appleseed) was a nurseryman who distributed chapters of *Heaven and Hell* to settlers in their cabins as he walked the midwestern frontier. By giving a few pages at a time, Johnny reached people who might not read a whole volume, and this was a way of giving them a glimpse of what he called "Good news, right fresh from heaven." Individuals who were receptive to the good news were often moved to share it with others, and some collaborated in doing so. In 1849 an organization was established with a purpose expressed in twelve words: "To encourage a wider circulation of the Theological Writings of Emanuel Swedenborg."

The organization was called The American Swedenborg Printing and Publishing Society. In 1928 the name was changed to the Swedenborg Foundation.

The Present Edition

OVER THE YEARS, the Swedenborg Foundation has kept Swedenborg's writings in print and available to the public; and *Heaven and Hell* has proved to be Swedenborg's most popular work. However, until 2002 the translation used most frequently had been done more than a century earlier. In 2002, a new translation of *Heaven and Hell* came out in a large, splendid edition complete with scholarly notes and presented in accessible modern English. Although it was a runaway bestseller, some readers found the size of the volume formidable. Therefore to satisfy demand for a smaller edition, the Foundation published the "Portable Edition," in smaller type size, which was welcomed particularly by those distributing the book in foreign lands. But the "portable" edition came to more than four hundred pages! Desiring to remove any barrier to accessibility to this work, the Swedenborg Foundation was motivated to commission a shortened version. The result is this book, *Afterlife: A Guided Tour of Heaven and Its Wonders*.

Using the translation of *Heaven and Hell* by George Dole for the New Century Edition of the Works of Emanuel Swedenborg, *Afterlife* contains direct quotations from *Heaven and Hell*, but they are selected quotations, not the complete work. Every chapter has been abbreviated, and some chapters have been omitted altogether. In addition, there is one important change in the sequence of the book. The original has three sections: the first about heaven, the second on the intermediate state immediately after death; and last about hell. The present volume, however, begins with the state immediately after death and then proceeds to heaven and hell, the sequence that a spirit follows in the afterlife.

And so the reader first encounters a chapter about the world of spirits, which is "where we first arrive after death," describing the experiences of a soul's awakening in the spiritual world. The next section, the main section of the book, is about specific aspects of heaven itself (in *Heaven and Hell*, the section on heaven comprises forty-three of the sixty-three chapters of the book). Since the first five chapters of the original *Heaven and Hell* have been omitted, I am providing a summary of their contents:

> The first chapter makes the basic statement that the God of heaven is the Lord Jesus Christ. He and "the Father" are one. He has "all power in heaven and on earth" (Matthew 28:18). He testifies that he is the resurrection and the life, and declares, "I am the way, the truth and the life."
>
> The second chapter states that, although heaven is made of angels, it is the divine nature of the Lord that really makes heaven. For this reason, angels take no credit for anything, ascribing all to the Lord.
>
> In the third chapter Swedenborg testifies, "All my experience in heaven bears witness to the fact that the divine nature that comes from the Lord, affects angels, and constitutes heaven is love. In fact, all the people there are forms of love and thoughtfulness. They look indescribably beautiful. Love radiates from their faces, from their speech, from every detail of their behavior."
>
> The fourth chapter shows the general division of heaven into two kingdoms, one kingdom of love composed of "heavenly angels." The other kingdom is of thoughtfulness

composed of spiritual angels.

The fifth chapter asserts that there are three heavens. "There is a central or third heaven, an intermediate or second one, and an outmost or first." This chapter ends with the disclosure of "a particular secret." Every angel and every one of us here on earth has a central or highest level; which is the Lord's gateway or his essential dwelling within us: "It is this central or highest level that makes us human and distinguishes us from the lower animals, since they do not have it. This is why we, unlike animals, can be raised up by the Lord toward himself, as far as all the deeper levels of our mind and character are concerned. This is why we can believe in him, be moved by love for him, and therefore see him. It is why we can receive intelligence and wisdom and talk rationally. It is also why we live forever."

The final paragraph of the fifth chapter reads as follows: "These, then, are some of the general facts. . . . In the following pages, we will need to say more about each heaven in particular."

Helen Keller, who took particular delight in *Heaven and Hell*, once spoke of experiencing a kind of joy when she read Swedenborg. You can compare your own experience, in which it is hoped you will find enlightenment, encouragement, and something of that joy.

DONALD L. ROSE, EDITOR

Preface

THE PARTICULAR HIDDEN contents to be disclosed in the pages that follow have to do with heaven and hell and with our own life after death.

Church people these days know practically nothing about heaven and hell or their life after death, even though there are descriptions of everything available to them in the Word. In fact, many who have been born in the church deny all this. In their hearts they are asking, "Who has ever come back to tell us about it?"

To prevent this negative attitude—especially prevalent among people who have acquired a great deal of worldly wisdom—from infecting and corrupting people of simple heart and simple faith, it has been granted me to be with angels and to talk with them person to person. I have also been enabled to see what is in heaven and in hell, a process that has been going on for thirteen years. Now I am being allowed therefore to describe what I have heard and seen, in the hopes of shedding light where there is ignorance, and of dispelling skepticism.

The reason this kind of direct revelation is taking place today is that this is what the Coming of the Lord means.

[EMANUEL SWEDENBORG, 1758]

xv

Part 1

THE WORLD OF SPIRITS
and
OUR STATE AFTER DEATH

What the World of Spirits Is

THE WORLD OF spirits is neither heaven nor hell but a place or state between the two. It is where we first arrive after death, being in due time either raised into heaven or cast into hell from it, depending on our life in this world. The world of spirits is a place halfway between heaven and hell, and it is also our own halfway state after death.

There is a vast number of people in the world of spirits, because that is where everyone is first gathered, where everyone is examined and prepared. There is no fixed limit to our stay there. Some people barely enter it and are promptly either taken up into heaven or cast down into hell. Some stay there for a few weeks, some for a number of years, though not more than thirty. The variations in length of stay occur because of the correspondence or lack of correspondence between our deeper and our more outward natures.

In the following pages I will be explaining just how we are led from one state into another and prepared.

After we die, just as soon as we arrive in the world of spirits, we are carefully sorted out by the Lord. Evil people are immediately connected with the hellish community their ruling love had affiliated them with in the world, and good people are immediately connected with the heavenly community their love and thoughtfulness and faith had affiliated them with in the world.

Even though we are sorted out in this way, we are still together in that world and can talk to anyone when we want to, to friends and acquaintances from our physical life, especially husbands and wives, and also brothers and sisters. I have seen a father talking with his six sons and recognizing them. I have seen many other people with their relatives and friends. However, since they were of different character because of their life in the world, they parted company after a little while.

However, people who are coming into heaven from the world of spirits and people who are coming into hell do not see each other anymore. They do not even recognize each other unless they are of like character because of a likeness in love. The reason they see each other in the world of spirits but not in heaven or hell is that while they are in the world of spirits they are brought into states like the ones they were in during their physical lives, one after another. After a while, though, they settle into a constant state that accords with their ruling love. In this state, mutual recognition comes only from similarity of love, for likeness unites and difference separates.

In these pages, where it says "spirits" it means people in the world of spirits, while "angels" mean people in heaven.

Each of Us Is Inwardly a Spirit

ANYONE WHO THINKS things through carefully can see that it is not the body that thinks, because the body is material. Rather, it is the soul, because the soul is spiritual. The human soul, whose immortality has been the topic of many authors, is our spirit; it is in fact immortal in all respects, and it is also what does the thinking in our bodies. The matter that is proper to the body is an addendum and almost an attachment to the spirit. Its purpose is to enable our spirit to lead its life and perform its services in a natural world that is material in all respects and essentially lifeless. Since matter is not alive—only spirit—we may conclude that whatever is alive in us is our spirit and that the body only serves it exactly the way a tool serves a live and activating force.

Since everything that is alive in the body—everything that acts and feels because of life—belongs to the spirit alone and none of it belongs to the body, it follows that the spirit is the actual person. In other words, we are essentially spirits and have much the same form as well. You see, everything that is alive and sensitive within us belongs to our spirit, and there is nothing in us, from head to toe, that is not alive and sensitive . This is why when our bodies are separated from our spirits, which is called dying, we still continue to be human and to be alive.

We may gather that inwardly we are spirits from the fact that after we depart from our bodies, which happens when we die, we are still alive and just as human as ever. To convince me of this, [the Lord] has allowed me to talk with almost all the people I had ever met during their physical lives, with some for a few hours, with some for weeks and months, and with some for years. This was primarily so that I could be convinced and could bear witness.

I may add here that even while we are living in our bodies, each one of us is in a community with spirits as to our own spirits even though we are unaware of it. Good people are in angelic communities by means of [their spirits] and evil people are in hellish communities.

Further, we come into those same communities when we die. People who are coming into the company of spirits after death are often told and shown this.

Our Revival from the Dead and Entry into Eternal Life

WHEN SOMEONE'S BODY can no longer perform its functions in the natural world in response to the thoughts and affections of its spirit (which it derives from the spiritual world), then we say that the individual has died. This happens when the lungs' breathing and the heart's systolic motion have ceased. The person, though, has not died at all. We are only separated from the physical nature that was useful to us in the world. The essential person is actually still alive. I say that the essential person is still alive because we are not people because of our bodies but because of our spirits. After all, it is the spirit within us that thinks, and thought and affection together make us the people we are.

We can see, then, that when we die we simply move from one world into another. This is why in the inner meaning of the Word, "death" means resurrection and a continuation of life.

The deepest communication of our spirit is with our breathing and our heartbeat; thought connects with our breathing, and affection, an attribute of love, with our heart. Consequently, when these two motions in the body cease, there is an immediate separation. It is these two motions, the respiratory motion of the lungs and the systolic motion of the heart, that are essential ties. Once they are severed, the spirit is left to itself; and the body, being now without the life of its spirit, cools and decays.

After this separation, our spirit stays in the body briefly, but not after the complete stoppage of the heart, which varies depending on the cause of death. In some cases the motion of the heart continues for quite a while, and in others it does not. The moment it does stop, we are awakened, but this is done by the Lord alone. "Being awakened" means having our spirit led out of our body and into the spiritual world, which is commonly called "resurrection."

The reason our spirit is not separated from our body until the motion of the heart has stopped is that the heart answers to affection, an attribute of love, which is our essential life, since all of us derive our vital warmth from love. Consequently, as long as this union lasts there is a responsiveness, and therefore the life of the spirit is [still] in the body.

I have not only been told how the awakening happens, I have been shown by firsthand experience. The actual experience happened to me so that I could have a full knowledge of how it occurs.

I was brought into a state in which my physical senses were inoperative—very much, then, like the state of people who are dying. However, my deeper life and thought remained intact so that I could perceive and retain what was happening to me and what does happen to people who are being awakened from death. I noticed that my physical breathing was almost suspended, with a deeper breathing, a breathing of the spirit, continuing along with a very slight and silent physical one.

At first then a connection was established between my heartbeat and the heavenly kingdom, because that kingdom corresponds to the human heart. I also saw angels from that kingdom, some at a distance, but two sitting close to my head. The effect was to take away all my own affection but to leave me in possession of thought and perception. I remained in this state for several hours.

Then the spirits who were around me gradually drew away, thinking that I was dead. I sensed a sweet odor like that of an embalmed body, for when heavenly angels are present anything having to do with a corpse smells sweet. When spirits sense this, they cannot come near. This is also how evil spirits are kept away from our spirit when we are being admitted into eternal life.

The angels who were sitting beside my head were silent, simply sharing their thoughts with mine (when these are accepted [by the deceased], the angels know that the person's spirit is ready to be led out of the body). They accomplished this sharing of thoughts by looking into my face. This is actually how thoughts are shared in heaven.

Since I had been left in possession of thought and perception so that I could learn and remember how awakening happens, I noticed that at first the angels were checking to see whether my thoughts were like those of dying individuals, who are normally thinking about eternal life. They wanted to keep my mind in these thoughts. I was later told that as the body is breathing its last, our spirit is kept in its final thought until eventually it comes back to the thoughts that flowed from our basic or ruling affection in the world.

Especially, I was enabled to perceive and even to feel that there was a pull, a kind of drawing out of the deeper levels of my mind and therefore of my spirit from my body; and I was told that this was being done by the Lord and is what brings about our resurrection.

When heavenly angels are with people who have been awakened they do not leave them, because they love everyone. But some spirits are simply unable to be in the company of heavenly angels very long, and want them to leave. When this happens, angels from the Lord's spiritual kingdom arrive, through whom we are granted the use of light, since before this we could not see anything but could only think.

I was also shown how this is done. It seemed as though the angels rolled back a covering from my left eye toward the center of my nose so that my eye was opened and able to see. To the spirit, it seems as though this were actually happening, but it is only apparently so. As this covering seemed to be rolled back, I could see a kind of clear but dim light like the light we see through our eyelids when we are first waking up. It seemed to me as though this clear, dim light had a heavenly color to it, but I was later told that this varies. After that, it felt as though something were being rolled gently off my face, and once this was done I had access to spiritual thought. This rolling something off the face is an appearance, for it represents the fact that we are moving from natural thinking to spiritual thinking. Angels take the greatest care to shield the awakening person from any concept that does not taste of love. Then they tell the individual that he or she is a spirit.

After the spiritual angels have given us the use of light, they do everything for us as newly arrived spirits that we could ever wish in that state. They tell us—at least to the extent that we can grasp it— about the realities of the other life. However, if our nature is such that we do not want to be taught, then once we are awakened we want to get out of the company of angels. Still, the angels do not leave us, but we do leave them. Angels really do love everyone. They want nothing more than to help people, to teach them, to lead them into heaven. This is their highest joy.

When spirits leave the company of angels, they are welcomed by the good spirits who are accompanying them and who also do all they can for them. However, if they had led the kind of life in the world that makes it impossible for them to be in the company of good people, then they want to get away from these as well. This happens as long and as many times as necessary, until they find the company of people their earthly life has fitted them for. Here they find their life; and remarkable as it may sound, they then lead the same kind of life they had led in the world.

This first stage of our life after death does not last more than a few days, though. In the following pages I will be describing how we are then brought from one state into another until finally we arrive either in heaven or in hell.

I have talked with some people on the third day after their death. I talked with three whom I had known in the world and told them that their funeral services were now being planned so that their bodies could be buried. When they heard me say it was so that they could be buried, they were struck with a kind of bewilderment. They said that they were alive, and that people were burying what had been useful to them in the world. Later on, they were utterly amazed at the fact that while they had been living in their bodies they had not believed in this kind of life after death, and particularly that this was the case for almost everyone.

After Death, We Are in a Complete Human Form

YEARS AND YEARS of daily experience have witnessed to me that after separation from the body the human spirit is a person and is in a similar form. I have seen this thousands of times, I have heard such spirits, and I have talked with them even about the fact that people in the world do not believe that they are what they are, and that scholars think people who do believe are simpletons. Spirits are heartsick over the fact that this kind of ignorance is still common in the world and especially in the church.

This is why almost all the people who arrive from this world are as astonished as they can be to find that they are alive and that they are just as human as ever, that they are seeing and hearing and talking, that their bodies are still endowed with the sense of touch, and that nothing at all has changed.

When we first enter the world of spirits (which happens shortly after the reawakening just described), our spirit has a similar face and tone of voice as it did in the world. This is because at that point we are in the state of our external concerns, with our deeper concerns not yet uncovered. This is our initial state after decease. Later, though, our face changes and becomes quite different. It comes to look like the ruling affection in which the deeper reaches of our minds were engaged in the world, the kind of affection characteristic of the spirit within our body, because the face of our spirit is very different from the face of our body. We get our physical face from our parents and our spiritual face from our affection, which it images. Our spirit takes on this face after our physical life is over, when the outer coverings have been removed. This is our third state.

11

I have seen some newcomers from the world and have recognized them by their faces and voices; but when I saw them later, I did not recognize them. People who were engaged in good affections had lovely faces, while people who were engaged in evil affections had ugly ones. Seen in its own right, our spirit is nothing but our affections, whose outward form is our face.

The reason our faces change is that in the other life no one is allowed to pretend to affections they do not really have, so we cannot put on a face that is contrary to the love we are engaged in. We are all refined down to a state in which we say what we think and manifest in expression and act what we intend.

It does need to be known that our human form is lovelier after death to the extent that we have more deeply loved divine truths and have lived by them, since our deeper levels are opened and formed according to both our love of these truths and our life. So the deeper the affection and the more it accords with heaven, the lovelier the face. This is why the angels who are in the inmost heaven are the loveliest—because they are forms of heavenly love. On the other hand, people who have loved divine truths more outwardly and have therefore lived by them more outwardly are less lovely, since only the more outward aspects radiate from their faces, and the deeper heavenly love—which means the form of heaven as it is in its own right—does not shine through these more outward forms. You can see something relatively dim in their faces, not enlivened by a light of their inner life shining through. In short, all perfection increases as you move inward and lessens as you move outward. As the perfection increases or lessens, so does the beauty.

I have seen faces of angels of the third heaven so beautiful that no painters, with all their skill, could render a fraction of their light with their pigments or rival a thousandth part of the light and life that show in their faces. The faces of angels of the outmost heaven, though, can be mirrored to some extent.

Finally, I should like to offer a secret no one has ever known before, namely that everything good and true that comes from the Lord and makes heaven is in the human form. This is true not only of the greatest whole but also of every least part. This form influences everyone who accepts what is good and true from the Lord, and causes everyone in heaven to be in a human form according to that acceptance. This is why heaven is consistent with itself in general and in particular, why the human form is the form of the whole, of each community, and of each angel. I need to add here that this is also the form of the details of thought that come from heavenly love in angels.

This secret may not fit well into the understanding of anyone on earth, but it is clear to the understanding of angels because they are in heaven's light.

After Death, We Enjoy Every Sense, Memory, Thought, and Affection We Had in the World

REPEATED EXPERIENCE HAS witnessed to me that when we move from the natural world into the spiritual, which happens when we die, we take with us everything that pertains to our character except our earthly body. In fact, when we enter the spiritual world or our life after death, we are in a body as we were in this world. There seems to be no difference, since we do not feel or see any difference. This body is spiritual, though, so it has been separated or purified from earthly matter. Further, when anything spiritual touches and sees something spiritual, it is just like something natural touching and seeing something natural. So when we have become a spirit, we have no sense that we are not in the body we inhabited in the world, and therefore do not realize that we have died.

As "spirit-people," we enjoy every outer and inner sense we enjoyed in the world. We see the way we used to; we hear and talk the way we used to; we smell and taste and feel things when we touch them the way we used to; we want, wish, crave, think, ponder, are moved, love, and intend the way we used to. Studious types still read and write as before. In a word, when we move from the one life into the other, or from the one world into the other, it is like moving from one [physical] place to another; and we take with us everything we owned as persons to the point that it would be unfair to say that we have lost anything of our own after death, which is only a death of the earthly body. We even take with us our natural memory, since we retain everything we have heard, seen, read, learned, or thought in the world from earliest infancy to the very end of life. However, since the natural objects that reside in our memory cannot be reproduced in a spiritual world, they become dormant the way they do when we are not thinking about them. Even so, they can be reproduced when it so pleases the Lord. I will have more to say soon, though, about this memory and its condition after death.

Nevertheless, the difference between our life in the spiritual world and our life in the natural world is considerable, in regard both to our outer senses and the way they affect us and to our inner senses and the way they affect us. People who are in heaven have far more delicate senses. That is, they see and hear and also think more discerningly than when they were in this world. This is because they are seeing in heaven's light, which vastly surpasses the world's light, and they hear by way of a spiritual atmosphere that vastly surpasses the atmosphere of the earth. The difference in their outer senses is like that between something clear and something hidden by a cloud, or like noonday light and the dimness of evening.

As for our keeping our whole memory when we leave the world, I have been shown this by many examples and have seen and heard a great deal worth talking about. I should like to cite a few examples in a sequence. There have been people who denied the crimes and transgressions they had committed in the world. To prevent them from believing they were blameless, everything was disclosed and drawn out of their own memory in sequence from the beginning of their life to the end. Most of these transgressions were acts of adultery and promiscuity.

There were people who had deceived others with malicious skill and had stolen from them. Their deceptions and thefts were also recounted one after the other, many of them known to practically no one in the world other than themselves. They even admitted them because they were made plain as day, along with every thought, intention, pleasure, and fear that mingled in their minds at the time.

There were people who had taken bribes and made money from judicial decisions. They were similarly examined from their own memories, and everything was recounted from their first taking office to the end. The details of amount and value, of the time, and of their state of mind and intention, all consigned to their remembrance together, were brought to view, a hundred or more instances. In some cases, remarkably enough, the very diaries in which they had recorded these deeds were opened and read to them, page by page.

There were men who had lured virgins to dishonor and violated their chastity. They were summoned to a similar judgment, and the details were drawn out of their memory and listed. The actual faces of the virgins and other women were presented as though they were there in person, along with the places, the words, and the thoughts. It was done as instantaneously as when something is actually being witnessed firsthand. Sometimes these presentations lasted for hours.

There was one man who thought nothing of slandering others. I heard his slanders recounted in sequence as well as his blasphemies, along with the actual words, the people they were about, and the people they were addressed to. All these were presented together as lifelike as could be even though he had very carefully kept them hidden from his victims while he was living in the world.

There was one man who had defrauded a relative of his legacy by some devious pretext. He was exposed and judged in the same way. Remarkably, the letters and documents they exchanged were read aloud to me, and he said that not a word was missing. This same man had also secretly killed a neighbor by poison just before his own death, which was disclosed in the following way. A trench seemed to open under his feet, and as it was opened, a man came out as though from a tomb and screamed at him, "What have you done to me?" Then everything was disclosed—how the poisoner had talked amicably with him and offered him a drink, what he had thought beforehand, and what happened afterward. Once this was uncovered, the murderer was condemned to hell.

In a word, all their evils, crimes, thefts, wiles, and deceptions are made clear to every evil spirit. They are drawn from their own memories and exposed. There is no room for denial because all the circumstances are presented together.

I also heard that angels have seen and displayed from the memory of one individual everything he had thought one day after another over the course of a month, with never an error, recalled as though he himself were back in those very days.

We may gather from these instances that we take our whole memory with us, and that nothing is so concealed in this world that it will not be made known after death, made known in public.

When we are being faced with our deeds after death, angels who have been given the task of examining look searchingly into the face and continue their examination through the whole body, beginning with the fingers first of one hand and then of the other and continuing through the whole. When I wondered why this was so, it was explained to me. The reason is that just as the details of our thought and intention are inscribed on our brains because that is where their beginnings are, so they are inscribed on the whole body as well, since all the elements of our thought and intention move out into the body from their beginnings and take definition there in their outmost forms. This is why the things that are inscribed on our memory from our intention and consequent thought are inscribed not only on the brain but also on the whole person, where they take form in a pattern that follows the pattern of the parts of the body. I could therefore see that our overall nature depends on the nature of our intention and consequent thought, so that evil people are their own evil and good people are their own good.

We may also gather from this what is meant by our book of life, mentioned in the Word. It is the fact that all our deeds and all our thoughts are written on our whole person and seem as though they are read from a book when they are called out of our memory. They appear in a kind of image when our spirit is looked at in heaven's light.

I should like to add to this something noteworthy about the memory that we keep after death, something that convinced me that not just the general contents but even the smallest details that have entered our memory do last and are never erased. I saw some books with writing in them like earthly writing, and was told that they had come from the memories of the people who had written them, that not a single word was missing that had been in the book they had written in the world. I was also told that all the least details could be retrieved from the memory of someone else, even things the person had forgotten in the world. The reason for this was explained as well; namely, that we have an outer and an inner memory, the outer proper to our natural person and the inner proper to our spiritual person. The details of what we have thought, intended, said, and done, even what we have heard and seen, are inscribed on our inner or spiritual memory. There is no way to erase anything there, since everything is written at once on our spirit itself and on the members of our body, as noted above. This means that our spirit is formed in accord with what we have thought and what we have done intentionally. I know these things seem paradoxical and hard to believe, but they are true nevertheless.

Let no one believe, then, that there is anything we have thought or done in secret that will remain hidden after death. Believe rather that absolutely everything will come out into broad daylight.

I have talked with any number of people who were regarded as learned in the world because of their knowledge of such ancient languages as Hebrew and Greek and Latin, but who had not developed their rational functioning by means of the things that were written in those languages. Some of them seemed as simple as people who did not know anything about those languages; some of them seemed dense, though there still remained a pride, as though they were wise than other people.

Spirits and angels have memory just as we do. What they hear and see and think and intend and do stays with them; and through their memory they are constantly developing their rational ability forever. This is why spirits and angels are being perfected in intelligence and wisdom through experiences of what is true and good just the way we are.

I have been shown that spirits and angels have memory by a great deal of experience as well. I have seen everything they had thought and done called up from their memory both in public and in private, when they were with other spirits. I have also seen people who had been focused on some truth from simple virtue become steeped in insights and in a consequent intelligence and then taken up into heaven.

It should be realized, though, that they are not steeped in insights and a consequent intelligence beyond the level of the affection for what is good and true that engaged them in the world. In fact, each spirit and angel retains the amount and kind of affection she or he had in the world, and this is afterward perfected by being filled in. This too goes on forever, since everything is capable of infinite variation and enrichment by different means, so it can be multiplied and can bear fruit. There is no end to any instance of goodness, since its source is the Infinite.

Our Nature after Death Depends on the Kind of Life We Led in the World

ANY CHRISTIAN KNOWS from the Word that our life is still with us after death, since it says in many places that we will be judged according to our deeds and works and rewarded accordingly. Further, anyone who thinks on the basis of what is good and from real truth cannot help but see that people who live well enter heaven and people who live evil lives enter hell. However, people who are intent on evil do not want to believe that their state after death depends on their life in the world. They think rather, especially when their health begins to fail, that heaven is granted to all on the basis of mercy alone no matter how people have lived, and that this depends on a faith that they keep separate from life.

It does say in many places in the Word that we will be judged and requited according to our deeds and works. I should like to cite a few passages here.

I will give to all according to their works. (Revelation 2:23)

I saw the dead, small and great, standing in the presence of God, and books were opened, and the dead were judged according to what was written in the books, according to their works; the sea gave up those who had died in it, and death and hell gave up the people who were in them, and they were all judged according to their works. (Revelation 20:13, 15 [20:12, 13])

Everyone who hears my words and does them I will compare to a prudent person, but everyone who hears my words and does not do them is like a foolish person. (Matthew 7:24, 26)

Jehovah deals with us according to our ways and according to our works. (Zechariah 1:6)

"Works and deeds," though, does not mean works and deeds solely the way they look in outward form. It also includes their deeper nature. Everyone knows, really, that all our deeds and works come from our intention and thought, for if they did not come from there they would be no more than motions like those of machines or robots. So a deed or work in its own right is simply an effect that derives its soul and life from our volition and thought. It follows, then, that the quality of the volition and thought that cause the deed or work determines the quality of the deed or work. If the thought and intent are good, then the deeds and works are good; but if the thought and intent are evil, then the deeds and works are evil, even though they may look alike in outward form. A thousand people can behave alike—that is, can do the same thing, so much alike that in outward form one can hardly tell the difference. Yet each deed in its own right is unique because it comes from a different intent.

Take for example behaving honestly and fairly with an associate. One person can behave honestly and fairly with someone else in order to seem honest and fair for the sake of self and to gain respect; another person can do the same for the sake of worldly profit; a third for reward and credit; a fourth to curry friendship; a fifth out of fear of the law and loss of reputation and office; a sixth to enlist people in his or her cause, even if it is an evil one; a seventh in order to mislead; and others for still other reasons. But even though all of their deeds look good (for behaving honestly and fairly toward a colleague is good), still they are evil because they are not done for the sake of honesty and fairness, not because these qualities are loved, but for the sake of oneself and the world, because these are loved. The honesty and fairness are servants of this love, like the servants of a household whom their lord demeans and dismisses when they do not serve.

We may gather from this what is meant by works and deeds in the Word.

A great deal of my experience has testified to the fact that *we are our love or intention after death.* All heaven is differentiated into communities on the basis of differences in the quality of love, and every spirit who is raised up into heaven and becomes an angel is taken to the community where her or his love is. When we arrive there we feel as though we are in our own element, at home, back to our birth-place, so to speak. Angels sense this and associate there with kindred spirits. When they leave and go somewhere else, they feel a constant pull, a longing to go back to their kindred and therefore to their dominant love. This is how people gather together in heaven. The same applies in hell. There too, people associate according to loves that oppose heavenly ones. Both heaven and hell are made up of communities and that they are all differentiated according to differences of love.

We may also gather that we are our love after death from the fact that anything that does not agree with our dominant love is then removed and apparently taken away from us. For good people, what is removed and apparently taken away is everything that disagrees and conflicts, with the result that they are admitted to their love. It is much the same for evil people, except that what is taken away from them is everything true, while for good people everything false is taken away. Either way, the result is that ultimately everyone becomes his or her own love. This happens when we are brought into our third state, which will be discussed below.

Once this has happened, we constantly turn our faces toward our love and have it constantly before our eyes no matter which way we face.

All spirits can be led wherever you want as long as they are kept in their dominant love. They cannot resist even though they know what is happening and think that they will refuse. Spirits have often tried to do something in opposition, but without success. Their love is like a chain or rope tied around them, with which they can be pulled and which they cannot escape. It is the same for people in this world. Our love leads us as well, and it is through our love that we are led by others. It is even more so when we become spirits, though, because then we are not allowed to present a different love or pretend to a love that is not ours.

We come into heaven if our love is heavenly and spiritual and into hell if our love is carnal and worldly without any heavenly and spiritual dimension. My evidence for this conclusion is all the people I have seen raised into heaven and cast into hell. The ones who were raised into heaven had lives of heavenly and spiritual love, while the ones who were cast into hell had lives of carnal and worldly love. Heavenly love is loving what is good, honest, and fair because it is good, honest, and fair, and doing it because of that love. If we love these things for their own sakes and do or live them, we are also loving the Lord above all because they come from him. We are also loving our neighbor, because these things are our neighbor who is to be loved. Carnal love, though, is loving what is good and honest and fair not for their own sakes but for our own sake, because we can use them to gain prestige, position, and profit. In this case we are not focusing on the Lord and our neighbor within what is good and honest and fair but on ourselves and the world, and we enjoy deceit. When the motive is deceit, then whatever is good and honest and fair is actually evil and dishonest and unfair. This is what we love within [the outward appearance].

Since these loves define our lives, we are all examined as to our quality immediately after death, when we arrive in the world of spirits, and we are put in touch with people of like love. If we are focused on heavenly love, we are put in touch with people in heaven; and if we are focused on carnal love, we are put in touch with people in hell. Further, once the first and second states have been completed the two kinds of people are separated so that they no longer see or recognize each other. We actually become our own love not only as to the deeper levels of our minds but outwardly as well, in face, body, and speech. People who are carnal loves look coarse, dim, dark, and misshapen; while people who are heavenly loves look lively, clear, bright, and lovely.

Our First State after Death

THERE ARE THREE states that we pass through after death before we arrive in either heaven or hell. The first state is one of more outward concerns, the second is one of more inward concerns, and the third is one of preparation. We go through these states in the world of spirits.

Some people, however, do not go through these states but are either raised into heaven or cast into hell immediately after their death. The people immediately raised into heaven are ones who have been regenerated and thus prepared for heaven in this world. People who have been regenerated and prepared to this extent need only to slough off their natural uncleanness along with their bodies and are immediately taken into heaven by angels. I have seen people taken up an hour after their death.

On the other hand, people who have been profoundly malicious but have outwardly worn a guise of goodness, people who have therefore filled their malice with guile and used goodness as a means of deception are cast directly into hell. I have seen people like this cast into hell immediately after their death. One of the most deceitful went head first and feet last; for others it is different.

There are also people who are sent off into caves right after their death and in this way are segregated from people in the world of spirits. They are alternately brought out and sent back in. These are people who have treated their neighbors maliciously under the pretext of civic behavior.

There are few such people, though, compared to the number of people who are kept in the world of spirits and prepared there for either heaven or hell according to the divine plan.

As to the first state, the state of more outward concerns, we arrive in this immediately after our death. Everyone has more outward and inward aspects of the spirit. We use the outer aspects of our spirit to adapt our bodies in the world—especially our faces, speech, and behavior—to our interactions with other people. The more inward aspects of our spirit are the ones proper to our intentions and consequent thought, which rarely show in our faces, speech, and behavior. We are trained from infancy to present ourselves as friendly, benevolent, and honest, and to conceal the thoughts of our own intentions. So we acquire a habitual lifestyle that is outwardly moral and civil no matter what we are like inwardly. As a result of this habitual behavior, we scarcely know our own inner natures and pay no attention to them.

Our first state after death is like our state in this world, since we are then similarly involved in outward concerns. We have similar faces, voices, and character; we lead similar moral and civil lives. This is why it still seems to us as though we were in this world unless we notice things that are out of the ordinary and remember that angels told us we were spirits when we were awakened. So the one life carries on into the other, and death is only a passage.

Since this is what we are like as spirits immediately after our life in the world, our friends and people we had known in the world then recognize us. Spirits perceive who we are not only from our faces and voices but also from the aura of our life when they come near. In the other life, whenever we think about someone, we call up that individual's face in our thought along with many details about her or his life; and when we do this, the other is called to us. Things like this happen in the spiritual world because thoughts are shared there and because space is not what it is in the natural world. This is why as soon as we arrive in the other life, we are all recognized by our friends and relatives and by people we have known in one way or another. Further, we talk with each other and continue to see each other in keeping with our friendship in the world. I have heard many people who had just come from the world overjoyed to see their friends again, and their friends overjoyed that they had arrived.

It often happens that married partners meet and welcome each other joyfully. They stay together as well, but for a longer or shorter time depending on how happily they had lived together in the world. Ultimately, unless they had been united by real marriage love (which is a union of minds from heavenly love), they separate after having been together for a while.

If the minds of the partners disagreed, however, and if they were inwardly repellent to each other, they break out into open hostility and sometimes actually fight with each other. Still, they are not

27

separated until they enter the second state, which will be described shortly.

Since the life of newly arrived spirits is not unlike their life in the world, and since they do not know anything about life after death, heaven, or hell except what they have learned from the literal meaning of the Word and some sermons drawn from it, once they get over their astonishment at being in a body and enjoying all the senses they had in the world, seeing familiar things around them, they find themselves wanting to know what heaven and hell are like and where they are. Consequently, their friends tell them about the state of eternal life and take them around to various places, into the company of different people. They go to different cities, to gardens and parks. Then from time to time they are led into the thoughts they had had during their physical lives about the state of the soul after death and about heaven and hell. This brings them to the point of resentment that they had been so ignorant about such matters, and also that the church had been so ignorant.

Almost all of them want to know whether they will make it into heaven. Many of them think they will because they led moral and civic lives in the world, not reflecting that both evil and good people lead similar outward lives, being similarly helpful to others, going to church, listening to sermons, and praying similarly, utterly unaware that outward behavior and outward worship accomplish nothing whatever; only the inner realities that give rise to these outward ones are effective. Scarcely one in thousands even knows what the inner realities are or that they are the focal point of heaven and the church for us. Even fewer realize that the quality of our outward actions is determined by the quality of our intentions and thoughts and the love and faith within them, from which our actions arise. Even when they are told, they do not grasp the fact that thinking and intending actually make a difference. They attach importance only to speaking and acting. Many of the people who are coming into the other life from the Christian world are like this nowadays.

All the spirits who arrive from the world are put in touch with some community in heaven or some community in hell. However, this applies only to their deeper natures, and their deeper natures are not apparent to them as long as they are focused on their outward concerns. This is because their outward concerns cloak their inner ones, especially for people more deeply involved in evil. However, they come out in the open when they arrive in the second state because there their deeper levels are opened and their outer ones become dormant.

This first state after death lasts a few days for some people, months for some, and a year for some, but rarely more than a year for anyone. The difference for particular individuals depends on the harmony or discord between their inner and outer natures. No one is allowed to think and intend one way and speak and act another way in the spiritual world. Everyone must be an image of his or her affection or love, which means we must be outwardly what we are inwardly. This is why the outer concerns of a spirit are first stripped off and brought into order: so that they may serve as a plane responsive to the inner ones.

Our Second State after Death

Our second state after death is called a state of our deeper interests because then we are given access to the deeper reaches of our minds, or of our intentions and thoughts, while the more outward interests that engaged us in the first state become dormant.

Anyone who is observant of our life and our words and actions can recognize that we all have more outward and more inward natures, or more outward and more inward thoughts and intentions. We can recognize this from the fact that if we are involved in civic life, we think about other people in terms of their reputation, or of what we have picked up about them when they were the subjects of conversation. However, we do not talk with them the way we think about them, and even if the others are evil people, we still behave courteously toward them. This is particularly noticeable in pretenders and sycophants whose words and deeds are wholly at odds with their thoughts and intentions, and in hypocrites who talk about God, heaven, the salvation of souls, the truths of the church, the welfare of the country, and their neighbor as though they were motivated by faith and love when at heart they believe otherwise and love no one but themselves.

We need to know that our basic quality is determined entirely by the quality of our inner natures, not by what we are like outwardly apart from that inner nature. This is because our inner reaches are our spirit, and since it is from the spirit that the body lives, our life is the life of our spirit. Consequently, whatever we are like in our inward natures, that is what we are like to eternity. Since our more outward natures belong to the body they are separated after death, and any elements of them that cling to the spirit become dormant, serving only as a plane for deeper concerns.

We can see from this what really belongs to us and what does not. For evil people the contents of the outer thought that gives rise to their words and the outer intent that gives rise to their actions do not really belong to them. What belongs to them is the contents of their deeper thought and intentions.

Once the first state has been completed—the state of more outward concerns described in the preceding chapter—we as spirits are brought into the state of our deeper concerns, or into the state of those deeper intentions and consequent thoughts we engaged in when we were left to ourselves in this world and our thinking was free and unfettered. We slip into this state without realizing it much as we did in the world when we drew the thought nearest to our speech, the immediate source of our speech, back toward our inner thought, and let it pause there a while. So when we as spirits are in this state, we are being ourselves and living our real life, since thinking freely from our own affection is our very life and our very self.

When spirits are in this state of their deeper concerns, then it is obvious what kind of people they really were in the world. They actually behave in accord with their own nature. People who were inwardly devoted to the good in the world then behave sanely and wisely, more wisely than when they were living in the world, in fact, because they have been freed from any connection with the body and therefore with the earthly things that darken and cover with a kind of cloud.

In contrast, people who were focused on evil in the world then behave foolishly and insanely, more insanely than when they were in the world, in fact, because they are in freedom and are no longer constrained. As long as they were living in the world, they were outwardly sensible, because this was how they imitated rational people. So when the outer layers are stripped off, their inner insanity is unveiled.

An evil person who outwardly pretends to be good can be compared to a brightly polished jar with a cover on, with all kinds of filth hidden inside, just as the Lord said: "You are like whitewashed sepulchers that look lovely on the outside but are inwardly full of the bones of the dead and all uncleanness" (Matthew 23:27).

When spirits are in this second state, they actually look exactly the way they were inwardly in the world. The things they had done and said in secret are made public, too, because now, since outward factors are not restraining them, they say the same things openly; and they keep trying to do the same things without any of the fear for the reputations that they had in the world. Further, they are then led into many states of their evils, so that they look to angels and good spirits like the people they really are.

Since evil spirits plunge into all kinds of evils when they are in this second state, it is normal for them to be punished often and severely. There are many kinds of punishments in the world of spirits, and there is no respect for rank, for whether someone was a king or a servant in the world. Every evil brings its own punishment with it. They are united; so whoever is involved in something evil is involved in the punishment of the evil as well. Still, no one suffers any punishment for evil things done in the world, only for current evil deeds. It boils down to the same thing, though, and makes no difference whether you say that we suffer punishments because of our evil deeds in the world or that we suffer punishments because of our evil deeds in the other life, because after death we all return to our life, which means that we are involved in the same kinds of evil. This is because our nature is determined by the kind of physical life we led.

The reason they are punished is that fear of punishment is the only means of taming their evils in that state. Encouragement does not work anymore, or teaching or fear of the law or fear for their reputation, because they are acting from their nature, which cannot be compelled or broken by anything but punishments.

Good spirits are never punished, though, even though they have done bad things in the world This is because their evils do not come back. I have also been granted a knowledge that their evils are of a different kind or nature. They do not stem from any deliberate resistance to what is true, and they are not from any evil heart except the one they acquired by heredity from their parents, which blind pleasure drove them into when they were involved in outward concerns separated from inner ones.

Every individual comes to the community where her or his spirit was in the world. Each of us, as to spirit, is actually united to some community, either heavenly or hellish, evil people to hellish communities and good people to heavenly ones.

33

Our Third State after Death Is a State
of Instruction for People Who Are Entering Heaven

OUR THIRD STATE after death, or the third state of our spirits, is one of instruction. This state is for people who are entering heaven and becoming angels, but not for people who are entering hell, because these latter cannot be taught. As a result, their second state is also their third, and ends in their turning straight toward their own love and therefore toward the hellish community that is engaged in a love like their own. Once this has happened, their intentions and thinking flow from that love; and since it is a hellish love, they intend only what is evil and think only what is false. These are their pleasures. Further, this results in their rejecting everything that is good and true that had served their love as means.

Good people, though, are brought from the second state into a third, which is a state of preparation for heaven by means of instruction.

Not everyone is taught in the same way or by the same communities of heaven. People who have been raised in heaven from infancy are taught by angels of the inner heavens because they have not absorbed false notions from distortions of religion or befouled their spiritual life with impurities drawn from rank and wealth in the world.

Most people who have died as adults are taught by angels of the outmost heaven because these angels are better adapted to them than are angels of the more inward heavens. These latter focus on a deeper wisdom that the deceased cannot yet accept.

Muslims, though, are taught by angels who once adhered to that religion but have turned to Christianity. Other non-Christians too are taught by their own angels.

All the teaching there is from doctrine drawn from the Word, and not from the Word apart from doctrine. Christians are taught on the basis of a heavenly doctrine that is in complete agreement with the inner meaning of the Word. The others, like the Muslims and non-Christians, are taught on the basis of doctrines suited to their grasp. These differ from heavenly doctrine only in that spiritual life is taught through a moral life in accord with the good tenets of their own religion, which was the basis of their life in the world.

Teaching in the heavens differs from teaching on earth in that [there] information is not consigned to memory but to life, since spirits' memory is in their life. They actually accept and absorb whatever agrees with their life and do not accept, much less absorb, what does not agree. This is because spirits are affections, and therefore have a human form that resembles their affections.

Since this is their nature, they are constantly breathing in a desire to know what is true, for the sake of constructive living. The Lord in fact sees to it that we love the constructive activities that suit our gifts. This love is intensified by our hope of becoming angels. This means that for each of us an affection for what is true is united to an affection for usefulness to the point that they act as one. A true understanding of use is sown in this way, so that the truths we learn are true perceptions of what is useful. This is how angelic spirits are taught and prepared for heaven.

There are various ways in which an affection for the truth suited to usefulness is instilled, many of them unknown in the world, primarily by depictions of useful activities. These can be presented in thousands of ways in the spiritual world, with such grace and charm that they permeate spirits all the way from the deeper levels of their minds to the outer levels of their bodies and therefore affect the whole person. As a result, spirits virtually become their constructive lives; so when they arrive in the communities their instruction has prepared them for, they are in their own life when they are engaged in their useful activities.

We may gather from this that awareness, which is an outward form of truth, does not get anyone into heaven. Rather, what gets us in is the useful life that is granted through knowledge.

After spirits have been prepared for heaven in these learning sites (which does not take long, because they are surrounded by spiritual concepts that comprehend a great deal at once), they are dressed in angelic clothing, usually white as linen, taken to a path that leads up toward heaven, and turned over to guardian angels there. Then they are accepted by other angels and put in touch with their communities and with a host of blessings. The Lord then takes each angel to her or his community. This happens in various ways, sometimes with detours. No angel knows the paths along which they are taken, only the Lord. When they arrive at their own communities, their inner natures are opened, and since they are in harmony with the inner natures of the angels who are members of that community, they are recognized instantly and accepted with joy.

It Is Not So Hard to Lead
a Heaven-Bound Life as People Think It Is

SOME PEOPLE BELIEVE it is hard to lead the heaven-bound life that is called "spiritual" because they have heard that we need to renounce the world and give up the desires attributed to the body and the flesh and "live spiritually." All they understand by this is spurning worldly interests, especially concerns for money and prestige, going around in constant devout meditation about God, salvation, and eternal life, devoting their lives to prayer, and reading the Word and religious literature. They think this is renouncing the world and living for the spirit and not for the flesh. However, the actual case is quite different, as I have learned from an abundance of experience and conversation with angels. In fact, people who renounce the world and live for the spirit in this fashion take on a mournful life for themselves, a life that is not open to heavenly joy, since our life does remain with us [after death]. No, if we would accept heaven's life, we need by all means to live in the world and to participate in its duties and affairs. In this way, we accept a spiritual life by means of our moral and civic life; and there is no other way a spiritual life can be formed within us, no other way our spirits can be prepared for heaven. This is because living an inner life and not an outer life at the same time is like living in a house that has no foundation, that gradually either settles or develops gaping cracks or totters until it collapses.

What follows will make it possible to see that it is not all that hard to lead a heaven-bound life.

37

Who can't lead a civic and moral life? After all, we are introduced to it in infancy and know it from living in the world. We do in fact lead this kind of life whether we are evil or good, since no one wants to be called dishonest or unfair. Almost everyone practices honesty and fairness outwardly, even to the point of seeming genuinely honest and fair, or seeming to act from genuine honesty and fairness. Spiritual people have to live in much the same way and can do so just as easily as natural people, the difference being that spiritual people believe in the Divine Being and act honestly and fairly not just because it follows civil and moral laws but also because it follows divine laws. In fact, since they are thinking about divine [laws] when they act, they are in touch with heaven's angels; and to the extent that they are, they are united to them, and their inner person—which is essentially a spiritual person—is opened. When this is our nature, the Lord adopts and leads us without our realizing it, and whatever things we do that are honest and fair—the deeds of our moral and civil life—come from a spiritual source. Doing what is honest and fair from a spiritual source is doing it from genuine honesty and fairness, or doing it from the heart.

The laws of spiritual life, the laws of civil life, and the laws of moral life are handed down to us in the Ten Commandments. The first three commandments contain the laws of spiritual life, the next four the laws of civil life, and the last three the laws of moral life. Outwardly, purely natural people live by these same commandments just the way spiritual people do. They worship the Divine, go to church, listen to sermons, wear devout faces, do not kill or commit adultery or steal or bear false witness, do not cheat their colleagues of their goods. However, they behave this way solely in their own interest, in order to look good in the world. Inwardly, these same people are exactly the opposite of what they seem to be outwardly. Because at heart they deny the Divine, they play the hypocrite in their worship. In their private thinking they scoff at the holy rites of the church, believing that they serve only to restrain the simple masses. This is why they are wholly cut off from heaven. So since they are not spiritual, they are not moral or civic people either; for even though they do not kill, they hate everyone who gets in their way and burn with vengefulness because of their hatred. So if they were not constrained by civil laws and the outward restraints exercised by their fears, they would kill. Because this is what they crave, it follows that they are constantly killing. Even though they do not commit adultery, still because they believe there is nothing wrong with it they are constantly adulterous, and actually do commit it as much as they can and as often as they have the opportunity. Even though they do not steal, still since they do covet other people's assets and regard cheating and malicious devices as legally justifiable, they are constantly stealing in their minds. The same applies to the other commandments of moral life—not bearing false witness or coveting the goods of others. All who deny the Divine are like this, all who do not have some conscience based on religion. Their nature shows obviously in similar people in the other life when they are let into their inner nature after their outer nature has been stripped away. Since they are separated from heaven at that point, they act in unison with hell; so they keep company with the people who live there.

It is different for people who at heart have acknowledged the Deity and have attended to divine laws in the deeds of their lives, living both by the first three commandments of the Decalogue and by the others as well. When they are let into their inner nature, after their outer nature is stripped away, they are wiser than they were in the world. Coming into their inner natures is like coming from darkness into light, from ignorance into wisdom, from a sad life into a blissful one, because they are in the Divine and therefore in heaven.

I have mentioned this to let it be known what each kind of person is like, though both may lead the same kind of outward life.

We can now see that it is not so hard to lead the life of heaven as people think, because it is simply a matter of recognizing, when something attractive comes up that we know is dishonest or unfair, that this is not to be done because it is against the divine commandments. If we get used to thinking like this, and from this familiarity form a habit, then we are gradually united to heaven. To the extent that we are united to heaven, the higher levels of our minds are opened, and to the extent that they are opened, we see what is dishonest and unfair; and to the extent that we see this, these qualities can be dispelled. For no evil can be banished until it has been seen. This is a state we can enter because of our freedom, since everyone is free to think in this way. However, once the process has started, the Lord works his wonders within us, and causes us not only to see evils but to refuse them and eventually to turn away from them. This is the meaning of the Lord's words, "My yoke is easy and my burden light" (Matthew 11:30).

It is important to realize, though, that the difficulty of think-ing like this and also of resisting evils increases to the extent that we deliberately do evil things—in fact, to that extent we become used to doing them until ultimately we no longer see them. Then we come to love them and to excuse them to gratify our love and to rationalize them with all kinds of self-deceptions and call them permissible and good. This happens, though, to people who in early adulthood plunge into all kinds of evil without restraint and at the same time at heart reject everything divine.

I was once shown the way to heaven and the way to hell. There was a broad path leading off to the left or north. There seemed to be a great many spirits traveling along it. In the distance, though, I could see a fairly large boulder where the broad path ended. Then two paths led off from the boulder, one to the left and the other, on the other side, to the right. The path to the left was narrow and con-fined, leading around through the west to the south, and therefore into the light of heaven. The path to the right was broad and open, leading obliquely down toward hell.

At first, everyone was clearly following the same path as far as the large boulder at the fork; but at that point they parted company. The good turned to the left and started along the confined path that led to heaven. The evil did not even see the boulder at the fork but fell over it and hurt themselves. When they got up, they rushed along the broad path to the right that led toward hell.

Later, the meaning of all this was explained to me. The first path, the broad one where so many good and evil people were traveling together, chatting with each other like friends with no visible difference between them, pictured people who live similarly honest and fair outward lives, with no visible difference between them. The stone at the fork or corner where the evil people stumbled, from which they rushed along the path to hell, pictured divine truth, which is denied by people who are focusing on hell. In the highest sense this stone meant the Lord's divine human nature. However, people who acknowledge divine truth and the divine nature of the Lord as well were taken along the path that led to heaven.

Paths in the other life picture the thoughts that flow from our aims or intentions. The paths that are presented to view there answer exactly to the thoughts of our aims, and our course follows the thoughts that flow from our aims. This is why you can tell the quality of spirits and of their thoughts from their paths. This also showed me the meaning of the Lord's words, "Enter through the narrow gate, for broad is the gate and open the way that leads to destruction, and there are many who walk along it; confined is the path and narrow the gate that leads to life, and there are few who find it" (Matthew 7:13–14). The way that leads to life is not narrow because it is difficult but because so few people find it, as stated.

The boulder I saw at the corner where the broad, common path ended and the two ways seemed to lead in opposite directions showed me the meaning of the Lord's words, "Have you not read what is written, 'The stone that the builders rejected has become the head of the corner'? Whoever falls over this stone will be shattered" (Luke 20:17–18). The stone means divine truth, and the rock of Israel means the Lord in regard to his divine human nature. The builders are the people of the church. The head of the corner is where the fork is, and to fall and be shattered is to deny and perish.

I have been allowed to talk with some people in the other life who had distanced themselves from the affairs of the world in order to live in devotions and sanctity, and also with some who had mortified themselves in various ways because they thought this was renouncing the world and taming the desires of the flesh. However, most of them had wound up with a gloomy kind of life from this and had distanced themselves from that life of active thoughtfulness that can be led only in the world, so they could not associate with angels. The life of angels is cheerful and blessed. It consists of worthwhile activities that are deeds of thoughtfulness. Particularly, people who have led a life withdrawn from worldly concerns are aflame with a sense of their own worth and constantly crave heaven. They think of heavenly joy as their reward, with no knowledge whatever of what heavenly joy actually is. When they are with angels and are let into that joy—which has no sense of merit and consists of activities and public duties and in bliss at the good that is accomplished through them —they are as bewildered as though they were seeing something totally alien to their faith. Since they are not open to these joys, they move off and associate with people who have led the same kind of life in the world.

There are other people who have lived outwardly devotional lives, constantly in churches and at prayer there. They have mortified their souls while constantly thinking about themselves, how they are worthier and more estimable than others and will be regarded as saints after their death. They are not in heaven in the other life because they have done all this with themselves first in mind. Since they have polluted divine truths by the self-love they immersed them in, some of them are so deranged that they think they are gods. So they are with similar people in hell. Some of them are ingenious and crafty and are in hells for the crafty people who used their skills and wiles to construct outward appearances that would lead the masses to believe them possessed of a divine sanctity.

I have mentioned all this to let it be known that the life that leads to heaven is not one of withdrawal from the world but a life in the world, and that a life of piety apart from a life of thoughtfulness (which is possible only in the world) does not lead to heaven at all. Rather, it is a life of thoughtfulness, a life of behaving honestly and fairly in every duty, every affair, every task, from our deeper nature and therefore from a heavenly source. The source of this life is within us when we act honestly and fairly because doing so is in accord with divine laws. ❧

Part 2

HEAVEN

The Heavens Are Made Up of Countless Communities

THE ANGELS OF any given heaven are not all together in one place, but are separated into larger and smaller communities depending on differences in the good effects of the love and faith they are engaged in. Angels engaged in similar activities form a single community. There is an infinite variety of good activities in heaven, and each individual angel is, so to speak, his or her own activity.

Kindred souls gravitate toward each other spontaneously, as it were, for with each other they feel as though they are with their own family, at home, while with others they feel like foreigners, as though they were abroad. When they are with kindred souls, they enjoy the fullest freedom and find life totally delightful.

We can see from this that the good gathers everyone together in the heavens, and that angels are differentiated by what good they do. Still, it is not the angels who gather themselves, but the Lord, the source of all that is good. He leads them, unites them, differentiates them, and keeps them in freedom to the extent that they are engaged in what is good. So he keeps every individual in the life of his or her own love, faith, intelligence, and wisdom—and therefore in happiness.

Further, people of similar quality all recognize each other there just the way people in this world recognize their neighbors and relatives and friends, even though they may never have seen each other before. This happens because the only relationships and kinships and friendships in the other life are spiritual ones, and are therefore matters of love and faith.

I have often been allowed to see this when I was in the spirit and therefore out of body and in the company of angels. Then some of them looked to me as though I had known them from infancy, while others seemed totally unfamiliar. The ones who looked as though I had known them from infancy were the ones who were in a state like that of my own spirit, while the unfamiliar ones were in dissimilar states.

All the individuals who make up a particular angelic community have a general facial resemblance, but differ in detail. I could grasp this general similarity and particular difference to some extent on the basis of similar situations in this world. We know that every race has a general similarity about the face and eyes that enables us to recognize it and distinguish it from other races, and that the same is even more true from one family to another. This holds true much more perfectly in the heavens, because there all the deeper feelings are visible and shine forth from the face, the face there being their outward and graphic form. It is not possible in heaven to have a face that differs from our feelings.

I have also been shown how this general similarity is varied in detail in the individuals of a single community. There was a kind of angelic face that appeared to me, and this was varied according to the qualities of affections for the good and the true that were characteristic of the individuals in a particular community. These variations lasted quite a while, and through it all I noticed that the same general face remained constant as a basis, with everything else being simply derivations and elaborations from it. In this way, too, I was shown the affections of the whole community that occasioned the differences in the faces of its members, for as already noted, the faces of angels are their deeper qualities taking form, which means they are forms of the affections proper to their love and faith.

We have noted above that there are larger and smaller communities in the heavens. The larger ones consist of tens of thousands of individuals, the smaller of some thousands, and the smallest of hundreds. There are even people who live alone, house by house, so to speak, and family by family. Even though they live apart, they are still arranged in the same pattern as those who live in communities, with the wiser of them in the center and the simpler at the periphery. They are very closely under the Lord's guidance, and are the best of angels.

Each Community Is a Heaven in Smaller Form and Each Angel a Heaven in Smallest Form

THE REASON EACH community is a heaven in smaller form and each angel a heaven in smallest form is that the activity of love and faith is what makes heaven. This good activity is in every community of heaven and in every angel of a community. It does not matter that this activity is different and distinctive everywhere, it is still the activity of heaven. The only difference is that heaven has one activity here and another there. So whenever anyone is raised into any community of heaven, they say that they are in heaven, each in his or her own. All the people who have arrived in the other life realize this; so individuals who are standing outside or below heaven and looking off into the distance where there is a gathering of angels say that heaven is there—and over there as well.

Just as a whole community is a heaven in lesser form, so too an angel is a heaven in least form. For heaven is not outside angels but within them. Their deeper levels, the levels of their minds, are arranged in the form of heaven and therefore are arranged to accept all the elements of heaven that are outside them. These elements they accept according to the quality of the goodness that is within them from the Lord. As a result, an angel is also a heaven.

It can never be said that heaven is outside anyone. It is within; because every angel accepts the heaven that is outside in keeping with the heaven that is within. We can see, then, how mistaken people are who think that getting into heaven is simply a matter of being taken up among the angels, regardless of the quality of their inner life, who believe that heaven is granted merely because of [the Lord's] mercy. On the contrary, unless heaven is within an individual, nothing of the heaven that is outside flows in and is accepted.

Since everyone accepts the heaven that is outside according to the quality of the heaven that is within, angels accept the Lord in the same way, because it is the Lord's divine nature that constitutes heaven. Consequently, when the Lord renders himself present in any particular community, his appearance depends on the nature of the good activity that community is engaged in. It is therefore not exactly the same in one community as in another. It is not that this difference is in the Lord: it is in the individuals who are seeing him from their own goodness and therefore in keeping with it. They are affected by the sight of him according to the quality of their own love. The ones who love him deeply are deeply moved, while the ones who love him less deeply are less deeply moved. Evil people, who are outside of heaven, find his presence intensely painful.

When the Lord does appear in any community, he appears there as an angel, but he is identified by the divine quality that shines through.

The Whole Heaven Reflects a Single Individual

IT IS A secret not yet known in this world that heaven, taken in a single all-inclusive grasp, reflects a single individual. In heaven, though, nothing is better known. Knowing this, knowing particulars and details about it, is the hallmark of angelic intelligence there. In fact, many other things follow from it and do not come clearly and distinctly to mind without this as their general principle. Since angels do know that all the heavens, like their communities, reflect a single individual, they refer to heaven as the universal and divine human—"divine" because the Lord's divine nature constitutes heaven.

Actually, angels do not see heaven in a single overview in this kind of form, since the entire heaven does not lie within the scope of any angel's sight. However, they do consistently see particular communities that are made up of many thousands of angels as single units in this kind of form; and from the community as a sample they draw their inference about the totality that is heaven. This is because in the most perfect form the greater elements are arranged like the parts, and the parts like the greater elements. The only distinction is between what is greater and what is lesser. Therefore they say that the entire heaven looks like this in the Lord's sight, because the Divine sees everything from the very center and summit.

Since heaven is of this nature, it is also governed by the Lord as though it were a single individual and therefore a single unit. We ourselves consist of countless different things, both overall and in our parts. We are made up overall of our limbs, organs, and viscera, and in our parts of series of nerves, fibers, and blood vessels—made up of members within members, then, and parts within parts. Still, we do of course recognize that when we do anything, we do it as whole individuals. This is what heaven is like, too, under the Lord's guardianship and guidance.

The reason so many varied elements act as one in an individual is that there is nothing whatever there that does not contribute something to the common good and do something useful. The inclusive body serves its parts and the parts serve the inclusive body because the inclusive body is made up of parts and the parts make up the inclusive body. So they provide for each other respectively, they focus on each other mutually, and they are united in the kind of form that gives every single component a relationship to the inclusive entity and its well-being. This is what enables them to act as a unit.

It is the same with assemblies in the heavens. People there unite in this kind of form in pursuit of any worthwhile activity. As a result any individuals who do not serve some use for the larger body are cast out of heaven because they are misfits. To "serve some use" is to intend well to others for the sake of the common good, while "not to serve some use" is to intend well to others not for the sake of the common good but for the sake of oneself.

Since heaven in its entirety does reflect a single individual, and is in fact the divine spiritual person in its greatest form and image, heaven is therefore differentiated into members and parts like a person, and these are given similar names. Angels know what member one community or another is in and say that this community is in the member or province of the head, that one in the member or province of the chest, that one in the member or province of the genitals, and so on.

In general, the highest or third heaven forms the head down to the neck, the middle or second forms the torso as far as the genitals and knees, and the lowest or first forms the feet to the very soles and also the arms all the way to the fingers, since the arms and hands are among our "lowest things" even though they are at our sides. We can see from this again why there are three heavens.

Each Community in the
Heavens Reflects a Single Individual

I HAVE BEEN allowed to see that a whole angelic community appears as a single entity in human form when the Lord makes himself present. High up toward the east, there appeared something that looked like a cloud, white at first and then reddening, surrounded by little stars. It came down, and as it gradually did so, it became brighter and finally took on a perfect human form. The little stars that surrounded the cloud were angels, who looked like that because of the light from the Lord.

We do need to realize that even though all the individuals in a community of heaven look like a single entity in human likeness when they are all together, still one community is not the same person as any other. They are differentiated like the faces of individuals of one lineage. The reason for this is that they differ depending on the various good activities that they participate in and that give them their form. Those communities that are in the central or highest heaven and are at its center appear in the most perfect and lovely human form.

It is worth noting that the more members there are in a single community and the more united they are in action, the more perfect is their human form. This is because variety arranged in a heavenly form makes perfection; and variety occurs where there are many individuals.

Every community in heaven is growing in numbers daily, and the more it grows, the more perfect it becomes. In this way, not only is the community perfected, but heaven in general is perfected as well, since the communities constitute heaven.

Since heaven is perfected by its numerical growth, we can see how mistaken people are who believe that heaven will be closed to prevent overcrowding. Actually, it is just the reverse. It will never be closed, and its ever increasing fullness makes it more perfect. So angels long for nothing more than to have new angel guests arrive there.

Every Angel Is in Perfect Human Form

LET US TURN to experience now. As for angels being human forms, or people, this I have seen thousands of times. I have talked with them face to face, sometimes with just one, sometimes with several in a group, and as far as their form is concerned, I have seen in them nothing different from that of a human being. At times I have felt surprised that they were like this; and to prevent it being said that this was some illusion or hallucination, I have been allowed to see them while I was fully awake, or while I was in full possession of my physical senses and in a state of clear perception.

I have often told them that people in the Christian world are in such blind ignorance about angels and spirits that they think of them as minds without form, as mere thoughts, and can conceive of them only as something airy with something alive within it. Further, since they attribute to them nothing human except a capacity for thought, they believe angels cannot see because they have no eyes, cannot hear because they have no ears, and cannot talk because they have no mouths or tongues.

Angels have replied that they know many people on earth have this kind of belief and that it is prevalent among the learned and strangely!—among the clergy. They have told me that it is because some of the learned who were particularly eminent and who came up with this kind of concept of angels and spirits thought about them on the basis of the sensory faculties of the external person. If people think on this basis and not on the basis of a more inward light and the common idea native to everyone, they cannot help constructing images like this, because the sensory faculties of the external person grasp only matters that are within the bounds of nature and not things that are higher. So they do not grasp anything at all about the spiritual world. From these eminent people as leaders, false thoughts about angels spread to people who did not think independently but relied on others; and people who let their thinking rely primarily on others and then form their faith, and later look into these matters with their minds, have a hard time giving these ideas up. As a result, many of them cooperate in confirming these false notions.

Angels have also told me that people of simple faith and heart are not caught up in this concept of angels, but have an image of them as people in heaven. This is because they have not let erudition snuff out the image implanted in them from heaven and because they do not grasp anything unless it has some form. This is why the angels we see sculpted and painted in churches are invariably represented as human. As for this "image implanted in them from heaven," angels tell me that it is something divine that flows into people who are intent on goodness of faith and life.

On the grounds of all my experience, which has lasted for several years now, I can say with full confidence that in their form, angels are completely human. They have faces, eyes, ears, chests, arms, hands, and feet. They see each other, hear each other, and talk to each other. In short, they lack nothing that belongs to humans except that they are not clothed with a material body. I have seen them in their own light, which is far, far greater than noonday on our earth, and in that light I have seen all the details of their faces more crisply and clearly than I have seen the faces of people here in the world.

I have also been allowed to see an angel of the central heaven. His face was more glorious, more radiant, than that of angels of the lower heavens. I looked at him very closely, and he had a human form in full perfection.

Some honest spirits I talked with about this were distressed at heart that there was such ignorance in the church about the state of heaven and about spirits and angels. They kept insisting that I should take back the message that they were not formless minds or ethereal breath but human in form, and that they saw and heard and felt just as much as people in this world do.

Owing to the Lord's Divine Human, Heaven, in Its Entirety and in Its Parts, Reflects a Person

THIS CONCLUSION—THAT it is owing to the Lord's divine human that heaven, in its entirety and in its parts, reflects a person—follows from all the things that have been presented [elsewhere]: (1) the Lord is God of heaven; (2) it is the Lord's divine nature that makes heaven; (3) the heavens are made up of countless communities, and each community is a heaven in smaller form and each angel a heaven in smallest form; (4) the whole heaven, grasped as a single entity, reflects a single individual; (5) each community in the heavens reflects a single individual; (6) therefore every angel is in perfect human form All these propositions lead to the conclusion that because the Divine is what makes heaven, the Divine is human in form.

The truth of this has been witnessed to me by an abundance of experiences, some of which now follow.

None of the angels in the heavens ever sees the Divine in any form except the human form. Even more remarkably, angels in the higher heavens cannot think about what is divine in any other way. They are led into the necessity of thinking this way because of the essential divine that is flowing into them and also because of the form of heaven, which determines how their thoughts reach out around them. In fact, all the thought that angels have spreads out in heaven, and they have intelligence and wisdom in proportion to this outreach. This is why everyone there acknowledges the Lord, since the divine human exists only in him. I have not only been told this by angels, I have been allowed to perceive it when I was raised into a more inward sphere of heaven.

We can see, then, that the wiser angels are, the more clearly they perceive this, which is why the Lord is visible to them. The Lord does appear in a divine angelic form, which is a human form, to people who acknowledge and trust in a visible Divine Being, but not to people who acknowledge and trust in an invisible Divine Being. The former can see the Lord's divine [form], but the latter cannot.

Since heaven in its entirety and in its parts does reflect a person because of the Lord's divine human, angels say that they are "in the Lord" and even that they are "in his body," meaning that they are in the very substance of his love. This is also what the Lord is teaching us when he says, "Abide in me, and I in you. As the branch cannot bear fruit on its own unless it abides in the vine, so neither can you unless you abide in me; for without me you can do nothing. Abide in my love. If you keep my precepts, you will abide in my love" (John 15:4–10).

Since this is how the Divine Being is perceived in the heavens, it is instinctive in everyone who accepts any inflow from heaven to think of the Lord in a human guise. The ancients did so and even modern people do, both outside and inside the church. Simple people see him in thought as an ancient one, in glory.

But this instinct has been stifled by all the people who have distanced themselves from the heavenly inflow by pride in their own intelligence and by evil lives. The ones who have stifled it by pride in their intelligence prefer an invisible God, while the ones who have done so by evil lives prefer no God at all. Because this instinct is not in them, neither type knows that it even exists, although this is the essential heavenly divine nature that flows into us first and foremost from heaven because we are born for heaven; and no one enters heaven without some concept of the Divine Being.

People in heaven are amazed that people here believe they are intelligent when they think of something invisible in the process of thinking about God, something that cannot be comprehended in any form, and that they call people who think otherwise unintelligent and even simpleminded, when the opposite is in fact the case. They assert that if people who regard themselves as intelligent on this account would examine themselves, they would find nature in the place of God for some, the nature in front of their eyes, for others, a nature they cannot see with their eyes. They would find that they are so blind that they do not know what God is, what an angel is, what a spirit is, what the soul is that will live after death, what the life of heaven is for us, or many other things that are matters of intelligence. Yet all the people whom they call simple know these things in their own way. They have an image of God as a Divine Being in human form, an image of an angel as a heavenly person, a concept of their soul that will live after death as being like an angel, and a concept of the life of heaven for us here as living by the divine commandments. Angels refer to these people as intelligent and fit for heaven, but the others they call unintelligent.

There Is a Correspondence of Everything in Heaven with Everything in the Human Being

PEOPLE TODAY DO not know what "correspondence" is. There are many reasons for this ignorance, the primary one being that we have moved away from heaven because of our love for ourselves and for the world. You see, people who love themselves and the world above all focus on nothing but earthly matters because these provide gratification to their more outward senses and pleasure to their moods. They do not attend to spiritual matters because these offer gratification to their deeper senses and pleasure to their minds. So they set such matters aside, saying that they are too lofty to think about.

The early people behaved differently. For them, knowledge about correspondences was the pearl of all knowledge. By means of it, they gained intelligence and wisdom, and by means of it those who were of the church had a communication with heaven. Knowledge about correspondences is in fact angelic knowledge.

The earliest ones, who were heavenly people, did their thinking from correspondence like angels, so they could even talk with angels. Further, the Lord was quite often visible to them, and taught them. Nowadays, though, this knowledge has been so completely lost that people do not know what correspondence is.

First, I need to state what correspondence is. The whole natural world is responsive to the spiritual world—the natural world not just in general, but in detail. So whatever arises in the natural world out of the spiritual one is called "something that corresponds." It needs to be realized that the natural world arises from and is sustained in being by the spiritual world, exactly the way an effect relates to its efficient cause.

By "the natural world," I mean all that extended reality that is under our sun and that receives its light and warmth from it. All the things that are sustained in being from that source belong to that world. The spiritual world, in contrast, is heaven, and to that world belong all the things that are in the heavens.

Since a human being is a heaven and a world in least form in the image of the greatest, there is a spiritual world and a natural world within each of us. The deeper elements, which belong to our minds and relate to our intelligence and volition, constitute our spiritual world, while the outer elements, which belong to our bodies and relate to our senses and actions, constitute our natural world. Anything that occurs in our natural world (that is, in our bodies and their senses and actions) because of our spiritual world (that is, because of our minds and their intelligence and volition) is called something that corresponds.

We can see in the human face what correspondence is like. In a face that has not been taught to dissimulate, all the affections of the mind manifest themselves visibly in a natural form, as though in their very imprint, which is why we refer to the face as "the index of the mind." This is our spiritual world within our natural world. Similarly, elements of our understanding are manifest in our speech, and matters of our volition in our physical behavior. So things that occur in the body, whether in our faces or in our speech or in our behavior, are called correspondences.

There Is a Correspondence
of Heaven with Everything Earthly

ALL EARTHLY THINGS are differentiated into three classes that we call "kingdoms," namely the animal kingdom, the vegetable kingdom, and the mineral kingdom. Members of the animal kingdom are correspondences on the first level because they are alive. Members of the vegetable kingdom are correspondences on the second level because they merely grow. Members of the mineral kingdom are correspondences on the third level because they neither live nor grow.

The correspondences in the animal kingdom are the living creatures of various kinds, both those that walk and creep on the earth and those that fly in the air. We need not list them by name, because they are familiar. Correspondences in the vegetable kingdom are all the things that grow and bloom in gardens and forests and farms and meadows, which again are so familiar that they need not be listed by name. Correspondences in the mineral kingdom are metals noble and base, stones precious and common, and soils of various kinds, as well as bodies of water. Beyond these, things made from these elements by human industry for our use are correspondences, things such as foods of all kinds, garments, houses, major buildings, and so on.

Things that are above the earth are also correspondences, things like the sun, the moon, and the stars, and also things that occur in our atmospheres like clouds, mists, rainstorms, lightning bolts, and thunderclaps. The emanations of the sun in its presence and absence like light and shade, warmth and cold, are also correspondences; and so are such corollaries as the times of the year called spring, summer, fall, and winter, and the times of the day—morning, noon, evening, and night.

The fact that everything in this world arises from the Divine and is clothed with the kinds of elements in nature that enable it to be present there, serve some use, and therefore correspond, follows clearly from little things we can observe in both the animal and the vegetable kingdoms. In each there are things that anyone, with some deeper thought, can see must come from heaven. By way of illustration I may mention only a few out of the countless many.

First, some from the animal kingdom. In this field, many people realize what kind of knowledge is virtually instinctive in any creature you choose. Bees know how to collect honey from flowers, build cells from wax in which they store their honey, and so provide food for themselves and their families for the coming winter. Their queen lays eggs, while the others cover them over and lead her around so that a new generation may be born. They live under a kind of government that all their members know instinctively, protecting their useful members and expelling the useless ones and clipping off their wings. There are even more marvels that are given them from heaven for their use. In fact, their wax serves the human race throughout the world for candles, and their honey for flavoring foods.

Then what about caterpillars, the lowest creatures in the animal kingdom! They know how to nourish themselves with the sap of their leaves and in due time how to make a covering around themselves and virtually put themselves in a womb and so to hatch offspring of their own species. Some first turn into nymphs and chrysalides and make threads, and after exhausting labor grace themselves with new bodies and adorn themselves with wings. Then they fly in the air as though it were their heaven, celebrate their "weddings," lay their eggs, and so provide themselves with a posterity.

Over and above these particular examples, all the fowl of the air know the foods that are good for them—not only what they are, but where they are. They know how to construct nests for themselves, each species differently from all others, how to lay their eggs there, incubate them, hatch and feed their chicks, and expel them from the nest when they can be on their own. They also know the particular enemies they must avoid and the allies they can associate with, all from earliest infancy. I will say nothing about the wonders in the eggs themselves, where everything necessary for the formation and nourishment of the embryonic chicks lies properly available, or countless other wonders.

Will anyone who thinks with any rational wisdom say that such things arise from any source but a spiritual world, a world that the natural world serves by clothing what comes from it with a body, or presenting in effect that which is spiritual in origin?

The reason why earthbound animals and the fowl of the air are born into all this knowledge while we, who are actually superior, are not, is that animals are in the proper pattern of their life and cannot destroy what is within them from the spiritual world because they are not rational. It is different for us, who think from the spiritual world. Because we have corrupted ourselves by living contrary to the design that reason itself has recommended to us, we cannot escape being born into total ignorance, so that we can be led from there, by divine means, back into the pattern of heaven.

We can deduce how members of the vegetable kingdom correspond from a multitude of instances—for example, from the fact that tiny seeds grow into trees, beget leaves, produce flowers and then fruits in which they place another generation of seeds, and that these things happen in a sequence and emerge all together in such a wondrous design that there is no way to describe it briefly. It would take volumes, and still there would be deeper mysteries suited to their uses that our knowledge could not compass.

Because these things stem from the spiritual world or heaven, which is in a human form, it is also true that the details of that kingdom have a kind of relationship to human characteristics—a fact that is recognized by some individuals in the learned world.

It has become clear to me from a great deal of experience that everything in that kingdom is also a correspondence. Very often, when I have looked over trees and fruits and flowers and vegetables in gardens, I have become aware of corresponding things in heaven. Then I have talked with nearby people there and have learned where these plants were from and what their characteristics were.

Nowadays, though, no one can know about the spiritual things in heaven to which natural things in the world correspond except from heaven, because the knowledge of correspondence has now been completely lost. I should like to present a few examples to show what the correspondence of spiritual things with natural ones is like.

In general, earth's living creatures correspond to affections, the mild and useful ones to good affections, the fierce and useless ones to evil affections. Specifically, cattle and calves correspond to affections of the natural mind, sheep and lambs to affections of the spiritual mind. Flying creatures, species by species, correspond to cognitive activities of either level of the mind. This is why various animals such as cattle, calves, rams, sheep, male and female goats, male and female lambs, as well as pigeons and turtle doves were accepted for holy use in the Israelite church, which was a representative church. They used them for their sacrifices and burnt offerings, and in these uses they did in fact correspond to spiritual realities that are understood in heaven in accord with their correspondence.

The reason animals are affections, according to their genera and species, is that they are alive, and the only source of the life of any creature is from affection and is in proportion to it. We humans are like animals as far as our natural person is concerned, which is why we are compared to them in colloquial usage. For example, we call a gentle person a sheep or a lamb, a violent one a bear or a wolf, a crafty one a fox or a snake, and so on.

There is a similar correspondence with things in the vegetable kingdom. A garden, in general terms, corresponds to heaven in respect to intelligence and wisdom, which is why heaven is called the garden of God and a paradise, and why we call it a heavenly paradise.

Trees, species by species, correspond to perceptions and first-hand knowledge of what is good and true, which yield intelligence and wisdom. So the early people, who were absorbed in the knowledge of correspondences, held their holy worship in groves. This is why trees are mentioned so often in the Word and why heaven, the church, and people are compared to them—to the vine, for example, the olive, the cedar, and others—and the good we do is compared to fruit.

Further, the foods we derive from them, especially the ones we get from crops planted in fields, correspond to affections for what is good and true because they nourish our spiritual life the way earthly foods nourish our natural life.

Bread, generally speaking, corresponds to an affection for whatever is good because it is the mainstay of life and because it is used to mean all food. It is because of this correspondence that the Lord calls himself the bread of life; and it is also because of this that bread was put to holy use in the Israelite church—they did in fact place bread on the table in the tabernacle and called it "the bread of presence." Then too, all divine worship that they performed by sacrifices and burnt offerings was called "bread." Because of this correspondence too, the most sacred worship in the Christian church is the Holy Supper, in which bread and wine are shared.

We may note briefly how the union of heaven with the world occurs by means of correspondences. The Lord's kingdom is a kingdom of purposes that are functions or—which amounts to the same thing—of functions that are purposes. For this reason, the universe has been so created and formed by the Divine that functions can clothe themselves in materials that enable them to present themselves in act or in results, first in heaven and then in this world, and so step by step all the way to the lowest things in nature. We can see from this that the correspondence of natural phenomena with spiritual ones, or of the world with heaven, takes place through functions, and that the functions are what unite them. We can also see that the forms that clothe the functions are correspondences and unions to the extent that they are forms of the functions.

As for us, though, our acts are services in forms to the extent that we live according to the divine design—that is, in love for the Lord and in thoughtfulness toward our neighbor. To that extent, our acts are correspondences that unite us to heaven. In general terms, loving the Lord and our neighbor is being of service.

We need to know as well that it is humankind through which the natural world is united to the spiritual world, that we are the means of the union. For there is within us a natural world and also a spiritual world; so to the extent that we are spiritual, we are a means of union. However, to the extent that we are natural and not spiritual, we are not a means of union. The Lord's inflow into the world and into the world's gifts within us continues even without our aid, but it does not come into our rational functioning.

The Sun in Heaven

OUR WORLD'S SUN is not visible in heaven, and neither is anything that is derived from it, since all that is natural. Nature, in fact, begins with that sun, and whatever is produced by it is called natural. The spiritual reality in which heaven exists, though, is above nature and completely distinct from anything natural. They communicate with each other only through correspondences.

However, even though neither this world's sun nor anything derived from it is visible in heaven, there is a sun there; there is light and warmth, there are all the things we have in our world and many more—not from the same origin, though, since things in heaven are spiritual while things in our world are natural.

Heaven's sun is the Lord; light there is the divine truth and warmth the divine good that radiate from the Lord as the sun. Everything that comes into being and manifests itself in the heavens is from this source.

The reason the Lord in heaven appears as the sun is that he is the divine love from which all spiritual things come into being—and, through the agency of our world's sun, all natural things as well. That love is what shines like a sun.

However, when the Lord appears in heaven (which happens quite often) he does not appear clothed with the sun but in an angelic form, distinguishable from the angels by the divine quality that shines from his face. He is not actually there in person—since the Lord "in person" is always clothed with the sun—but is present in appearance. It is commonplace in heaven for things to be seen as though they were present in the place where their appearance is focused or delineated, even though this is very far from the place where they themselves actually are. This presence is called "a presence of inner sight."

Since the Lord is the sun of heaven, and since everything that comes from him looks toward him, the Lord is the common center, the basis of all direction and orientation. So too everything beneath is in his presence and under his control, everything in the heavens and everything on earth.

Light and Warmth in Heaven

PEOPLE WHO THINK solely on the basis of nature cannot grasp the fact that there is light in the heavens; yet in the heavens there is so much light that it is vastly greater than noonday light on earth. I have seen it often, even during our evenings and nights. At first I was amazed when I heard angels saying that our world's light was nothing but shadow in comparison to heaven's light, but now that I have seen it, I myself can bear witness. Its brightness and brilliance are beyond description. What I have seen in heaven I have seen in that light, and therefore more clearly and distinctly than what I have seen in this world.

People are thinking naturally when they are focusing solely on this world and attributing everything to nature. They are thinking spiritually, however, when they focus on heaven and attribute everything to the Divine.

I have often been allowed to perceive that the light that illumines the mind is a true light, quite different from the light that we call natural light. I have also been allowed to see it. I have been gradually elevated into that light inwardly, and as I was raised up, my discernment was enlightened to the extent that I could grasp what I had been unable to grasp before, ultimately things that could in no way be comprehended by thought from natural light. At times I have resented the fact that they were incomprehensible [in natural light] when they were so clearly and plainly perceived in the heavenly light.

Since our mind does have light, we speak of it much as we do of our eyes—for example, that it sees and is in the light when it grasps something, and that it is in darkness and shadows when it does not; and there are many other similar sayings.

Something now needs to be said about heaven's warmth. In its essence, heaven's warmth is love. It emanates from the Lord as the sun, which is divine love for the Lord and from the Lord, as has been explained in the preceding chapter. We can therefore see that heaven's warmth is just as spiritual as its light, because they come from the same source.

There are two things that emanate from the Lord as the sun, divine truth and divine good. Divine truth comes out in heaven as light and divine good as warmth. However, divine truth and divine good are so united that they are not two, but one. For angels, though, they are separated. There are angels who accept divine good more readily than divine truth, and there are angels who accept divine truth more readily than divine good. The ones who are more open to divine good are in the Lord's heavenly kingdom; the ones who are more open to divine truth are in the Lord's spiritual kingdom. The most perfect angels are the ones who are equally open to both.

The fact that love is warmth of a spiritual origin can be seen from the way we grow warm in proportion to our love, even becoming inflamed and heated in proportion to its intensity and quality, with its full heat evident when we are attacked. This is why it is usual to talk about inflaming, heating up, burning, boiling, and kindling when we are talking about either the affections of a good love or the cravings of an evil love.

How the States of Angels in Heaven Change

ANGELS ARE NOT constantly in the same state as to love, and consequently they are not in the same state as to wisdom, for all the wisdom they have is from their love and in proportion to it. Sometimes they are in a state of intense love, sometimes in a state of love that is not intense. It decreases gradually from its most to its least intense. When they are in the highest level of love, they are in the light and warmth of their lives, or in their greatest clarity and delight. Conversely, when they are in the lowest level they are in shadow and coolness, or in what is dim and unpleasant. From this latter state they return to the first, and so on. The phases follow each other with constant variety.

These states follow each other like variations of light and shade, warmth and cold, or like the morning, noon, evening, and night of individual days in our world, varying constantly throughout the year. Not only that, they correspond—morning to the state of their love in clarity, noon to the state of their wisdom in clarity, evening to the state of their wisdom in dimness, and night to a state of no love or wisdom. It should be known, though, that there is no correspondence of night with the states of life of people in heaven, but rather a correspondence of the half-light that comes before dawn. The correspondence of night is with people who are in hell.

Because of this correspondence, "day" and "year" in the Word mean states of life in general, warmth and light mean love and wisdom, morning the first and highest level of love, noon wisdom in its light, evening wisdom in its shade, and the half-light the dimness that comes just before the morning. Night, though, means the loss of love and wisdom.

As the states of the inner levels of angels' love and wisdom change, so too do the states of the various things that surround them and are visible to their eyes; for the things that surround angels are given their appearance according to the things that are within them.

I have been told from heaven why changes of state like this occur. Angels have said that there are many reasons. First, the delight of life and of heaven that angels enjoy because of the love and wisdom given them by the Lord would gradually pall if they were constantly engaged in it, the way it happens for people who are involved in pleasures and enjoyments without variety. A second reason is that angels have a sense of self or self-image just as we do, and this involves loving themselves. All the people in heaven are kept free of their sense of self, and to the extent that the Lord does keep them free, they enjoy love and wisdom. To the extent that they are not kept free, however, they are caught up in love for themselves; and since all of them do love that sense of self and carry it with them, these changes of state or successive alternations do occur. A third reason is that they are made more perfect in this way, since they become accustomed to being kept in love for the Lord and kept free from love for themselves. Further, by these alternations of delight and discomfort, their perception of and sensitivity to what is good become more and more delicate.

They have gone on to say that the Lord does not produce these changes of their states, since the Lord as the sun is always flowing in with warmth and light, that is, with love and wisdom. Rather, they themselves are the cause, since they love their sense of self and this is constantly misleading them. They illustrate this by comparison with our world's sun, which is not the cause of the changes of warmth and cold and of light and darkness, of distinct years and distinct days, because it stays motionless. The reason can be traced to our earth.

When angels are in this last state, which is when they are involved in their sense of self, they begin to feel depressed. I have talked with them when they were in this state and witnessed their depression. They kept saying, though, that they lived in hope that they would soon return to their earlier state and be in heaven again, so to speak, since heaven for them is being kept free from their sense of self.

Time in Heaven

EVEN THOUGH THINGS keep happening in sequence and progressing in heaven the way they do in the world, still angels have no notion or concept of time and space. The lack is so complete that they simply do not know what time and space are.

The reason angels do not know what time is (even though everything for them moves along in sequence just the way it does in our world, so much so that there is no difference) is that in heaven there are no years or days, but only changes of state. Where there are years and days there are times, and where there are changes of state, there are states.

The reason we have times in our world is that the sun seems to move sequentially from one zone to another and to make the times we call the seasons of the year. It also moves around the earth and makes the times we call times of day, and it does these by fixed periods.

It is different for heaven's sun. It does not make years and days by sequential motions and rotations, but makes apparent changes of state; and it does not make these by fixed periods. This is why angels are incapable of having any concept of time, but have a concept of state instead.

It is much the same for all the things that occur as a result of time, such as the four seasons of the year called spring, summer, autumn, and winter; the four times of day called morning, noon, evening, and night; our own four ages called infancy, youth, maturity, and old age; and with the other things that either occur as a result of time or happen in temporal sequence. When we think about them, it is from a temporal standpoint; but an angel thinks about them from the standpoint of state. Consequently, anything in them that is temporal for us changes into an idea of state for the angel. Spring and morning change into an idea of love and wisdom the way they are for angels in their first state; summer and noon change into an idea of love and wisdom as they are in the second state; autumn and evening, as they are in the third state; and night and winter into a concept of the kind of state that is characteristic in hell. This is why similar things are meant by these times in the Word. We can see from this how the natural concepts that occur in our thought become spiritual for the angels who are with us.

Since angels have no notion of time, they have a different concept of eternity than we earthly people do. By "eternity," angels perceive an infinite state, not an infinite time.

I was thinking about eternity once, and using a concept of time I could grasp what "to eternity" entailed—namely, without end—but not what "from eternity" entailed and therefore not what God did before creation, from eternity. As my anxiety mounted because of this, I was raised into the sphere of heaven and therefore into the perception of eternity shared by angels. This shed light for me on the fact that we ought not to think about eternity in temporal terms but in terms of state, and that when we do, we can grasp what "from eternity" entails, which was actually done for me.

I have been allowed to know from experience what angels' ignorance of time is like. There was a particular individual from heaven whose nature did allow him to be let into natural concepts such as we have. I talked with him afterward, person to person, and at first he did not know what it was that I was calling "time." So I actually had to tell him how the sun seems to travel around our earth and make years and days, and that as a result, years are divided into four seasons and into months and weeks, and days into twenty-four hours, and that these times recur at fixed intervals. This gives rise to our expressions for time. He was astonished when he heard this, and said that he had not known that kind of thing, but only what states were.

In the course of our conversation I mentioned that it was known in our world that there is no time in heaven. We do actually talk as though we knew, since when people die, we say that they have left temporal things and have passed beyond time, meaning that they have left our world. I also said that it is known by some that times are states in origin because they recognize that times are experienced in precise accord with the states of affection we are caught up in. They are short for us when we are engaged in pleasant and cheerful pursuits and long when we are engaged in distasteful and depressing ones, and variable when we are in hope or expectation. As a result, scholars are asking what time and space are, and some of them even recognize that time is an attribute of the natural person.

A natural person may believe that we would have no thought if concepts of time, space, and matter were taken away from us, that all our thought is based on these foundations. Let such people know, though, that thoughts are limited and constrained to the extent that they derive from time, space, and matter, and that they are freed and expanded to the extent that they do not derive from such things, because to that same extent the mind is raised above bodily and worldly considerations. This is the source of angels' wisdom, which is so great that we must call it incomprehensible, since it does not fit into ideas that are formed merely from these [lower] concerns.

The Clothes Angels Appear In

SINCE ANGELS ARE people and live together the way people on earth do, they have clothes and homes and a great many other things: the difference, however, being that everything is more perfect for them because they are in a more perfect state. For just as angelic wisdom surpasses our wisdom so greatly as to be inexpressible, so too does everything that comes to their perception and sight, since everything perceived by and apparent to angels corresponds to their wisdom.

Like everything else, the clothes angels wear correspond, and since they do correspond they truly exist. Their clothes reflect their intelligence, so all the people in heaven are dressed according to their intelligence; and since one will surpass another in intelligence, one will have better quality clothing than another. The most intelligent wear clothes that gleam as though aflame, some radiant as though alight. The less intelligent wear pure white and soft white clothes that do not shine, and those still less intelligent wear clothes of various colors. The angels of the inmost heaven, though, are naked.

We can tell that angels' clothes do not merely look like clothes but really are because they not only see them, they feel them as well. Further, they have many garments that they take off and put on, and they put away the ones they are not using and put back on the ones they are. I have seen thousands of times that they wear different clothes.

I have asked them where they got their clothes, and they have told me that their clothes come from the Lord and are given to them, and that sometimes they are clothed without noticing it.

Angels' Homes and Houses

SINCE THERE ARE communities in heaven, with people living there the way we do, they too have homes; and these vary depending on the state of the life of each individual. They are splendid for people who are especially deserving and less splendid for people who are of lower rank.

At times, I have talked with angels about homes in heaven, telling them that nowadays hardly anyone would believe that they have homes and houses—some because they do not see them, some because they do not realize that angels are people, some because they believe that the angelic heaven is the sky they see about them with their eyes. Since this appears to be empty and they think that angels are ethereal forms, they come to the conclusion that angels live in the ether. Further, they do not grasp the fact that the same kinds of thing exist in the spiritual world as in the natural, because they know nothing about the spiritual.

But it would be better to present some experiential evidence at this point. Whenever I have talked with angels face to face, I have been with them in their houses. Their houses were just like the houses on earth that we call homes, but more beautiful. They have chambers, suites, and bedrooms in abundance, and courtyards with gardens, flower beds, and lawns around them. Where there is some concentration of people, the houses are adjoining, one near another, arranged in the form of a city with streets and lanes and public squares, just like the ones we see in cities on our earth. I have been allowed to stroll along them and look around wherever I wished, at times entering people's homes. This has happened when I was fully awake, with my inner sight opened.

The architecture of heaven is such that you might call it the very essence of the art—and small wonder, since the art itself does come to us from heaven.

Angels tell me that things like this and countless others even more perfect are presented to their view by the Lord; but that such sights actually delight their minds more than their eyes because they see correspondences in the details, and through their correspondences they see things divine.

The houses angels live in are not constructed as houses in our world are, but are given them by the Lord gratis, to each individual according to his or her acceptance of what is good and true. They also change slightly in response to the changes of state of their deeper nature.

Whatever angels possess, they attribute to the Lord, and anything they need is given to them.

Space in Heaven

EVEN THOUGH EVERYTHING in heaven appears to be located in space just like things in our world, still angels have no notion or concept of location and space. This can seem like a paradox, and since it is highly significant, I should like to shed some light on it.

All motion in the spiritual world is the effect of changes of inner states, to the point that motion is nothing but change of state.

This being the nature of motion, we can see that drawing near is likeness of inner state and moving away is dissimilarity.

This is also why in the spiritual world one individual is present to another if only that presence is intensely desired. This is because one person sees another in thought in this way and identifies with that individual's state. Conversely, one person moves away from another to the extent that there is any sense of reluctance; and since all reluctance comes from an opposition of affections and disagreement of thoughts, there can be many people appearing together in one place as long as they agree, but as soon as they disagree, they vanish.

Whenever people move from one place to another, whether it is within their town, in their courtyards, in their gardens, or to people outside their own community, they get there more quickly if they are eager to and more slowly if they are not. The path itself is lengthened or shortened depending on their desire, even though it is the same path. I have often seen this, much to my surprise.

We can see from all this again that distance and space itself depend wholly on the inner state of angels; and since this is the case, no notion or concept of space can enter their minds even though they have space just the way we do in our world.

We can illustrate this by our own thoughts, which are also devoid of space; for whatever we focus on intently in our thought is seemingly present.

The essential first cause of all this is that the Lord is present to each individual according to that individual's love and faith, and that everything looks near or remote depending on his presence, since this is what defines everything that exists in the heavens. This is what gives angels wisdom, since it provides them with an outreach of thoughts, which in turn affords them communication with everyone in the heavens. In a word, this is what enables them to think spiritually and not naturally, the way we do.

Forms of Government in Heaven

SINCE HEAVEN IS differentiated into communities, and the larger communities consist of some hundreds of thousands of angels, and since all the people in a given community are involved in similar good but not in similar wisdom, it follows of necessity that there are forms of government. Good order needs to be kept, and all matters of good order seen to.

The actual forms of government in heaven vary, though. There is one kind in the communities that constitute the Lord's heavenly kingdom and another in the communities that constitute the Lord's spiritual kingdom. They even vary depending on the particular function of each community. However, in the heavens there is no government except the government of mutual love, and the government of mutual love is heavenly government.

In the Lord's spiritual kingdom there are various forms of government, not the same in one community as in another but varying depending on the functions the communities fulfill. Their functions parallel those of the human [body], to which they correspond; and the variety of these is well known. The heart has one function, the lungs another, the liver another, the pancreas and spleen others, and so also for each sensory organ. Just as we have these various services going on in our bodies, so services are carried on in the universal human that is heaven, since it is its communities that correspond to them.

Still, all the forms of government share a central focus on the public good as their end, and within that good, the good of each individual. This is because everyone in all heaven is under the guidance of the Lord, who loves everyone and who from his divine love arranges things so that it is the common good from which individuals receive what is good for them. Each individual receives benefit in proportion to his or her love of the whole, for to the extent that they love the whole they love all the individuals. Since this love is the Lord's they are proportionally loved by the Lord and are benefited.

We may conclude from this what the officials are like—namely, that they are the people who more than others enjoy love and wisdom and who therefore, out of that love, wish well to everyone and out of that wisdom know how to make sure it happens. People like this do not control and command but minister and serve, for doing good for others out of a love for what is good is serving, and making sure that it happens is ministering. They do not make themselves more important than other people but less so, for they put the welfare of the community and of their neighbor first and their own later. What is first is more important, and what is later is less.

They do have respect and renown, though. They live in the center of their communities, loftier than others, and in splendid mansions as well; and they accept this renown and respect. However, they do so not on their own account but for the sake of obedience. They all know that this respect and this renown are gifts from the Lord, so that they may be obeyed.

This is the meaning of the Lord's words to the disciples:

Whoever among you wants to be great needs to minister to you; and whoever among you wants to be first needs to serve you. (Matthew 20:27–28 [26–28])

There are forms of government in the hells as well; for unless there were, they would not be kept in restraint. However, the forms of government there are exact opposites of those in the heavens because they all derive from selfishness. All people there want to control others and to be preeminent. They hate the people who do not agree with them, and use vicious means to get even with them because this is what selfishness is like. So for them it is the more vicious ones who hold office, and who are obeyed out of fear. But more on this later, where I discuss the hells.

Divine Worship in Heaven

OUTWARDLY, DIVINE WORSHIP in the heavens is not unlike divine worship on earth, but inwardly it is different. People there too have doctrines and sermons and church buildings. The doctrines agree in essentials, but those in the higher heavens are of deeper wisdom than those of lower heavens. The sermons are in keeping with the doctrines; and just as they have homes and mansions, they also have church buildings where the instruction takes place.

The reason things like this exist in heaven is that angels are constantly being perfected in wisdom and love. They have volition and intellect just as we do, and their intellect, like their intentions, is by nature constantly striving toward perfection—their intellect by means of the truths that constitute intelligence and their intentions through the values that constitute love.

All preachers are from the Lord's spiritual kingdom and none from his heavenly kingdom. The reason they are from the spiritual kingdom is that people there are attuned to truths that stem from what is good, and all preaching comes from truths. The reason none is from his heavenly kingdom is that the people there are attuned to the good of love, and see and grasp truths on this basis, but do not talk about them.

Even though the angels who are in the heavenly kingdom grasp and see truths, there are still sermons there because sermons are means of enlightenment in the truths that the angels already know and lead to further perfection by means of many things they have not known before. The moment they hear them, they acknowledge them and therefore grasp them. The truths they grasp they also love, and by living according to them they make them part of their life. They say that living by truths is loving the Lord.

All the doctrines that govern the preaching focus on life as their end, none on faith apart from life.

The Power of Heaven's Angels

PEOPLE WHO DO not know anything about the spiritual world and its inflow into the natural world cannot grasp the fact that angels have power. They think that angels cannot have power because they are spiritual and so pure and insubstantial that they cannot even be seen by our eyes. People who probe more deeply into the causes of things, though, feel otherwise about it. They are aware that all the power we ourselves have comes from our intellect and volition, since without these we cannot move the slightest part of our bodies. Intellect and volition are our spiritual person. This person is what animates the body and its members at will, for the mouth and tongue say what it thinks and the body does what it intends. It even bestows energy at will. Our intention and discernment are governed by the Lord through angels and spirits; and since this is true of our intention and discernment, it is true of all aspects of our bodies because these latter come from the former. Believe it or not, we cannot move a step without the inflow of heaven.

I have been shown that this is true by a great deal of experience. Angels have been allowed to activate my walking, my actions, my tongue, and my conversation as they wished, by flowing into my intention and thinking, and I learned at first hand that I could do nothing on my own. They told me later that everyone is governed in this way, and that we might learn this from the doctrine of the church and from the Word. We actually pray that God will send his angels who may lead us, guide our steps, teach us, and inspire us as to what we should think and say, and so on—this even though we talk and believe quite differently in our private thoughts apart from doctrine.

It does need to be known, though, that angels have absolutely no power on their own, but that all the power they have comes from the Lord. Further, they are powers to the extent that they recognize this fact. Any of them who believe that their power comes from themselves immediately become so weak that they cannot resist even a single evil spirit. This is why angels take absolutely no credit to themselves and turn down any praise or admiration for anything they have done, but attribute it all to the Lord.

The angels who constitute the arm in the universal human or heaven have the most power because they are the ones who more than any others are focused on things true, and good flows into their truths from the entire heaven. So too, all our strength is concentrated in our arms, and the whole body expresses its powers through them. This is why "arms" and "hands" in the Word mean power.

Sometimes a bare arm appears in heaven that has so much power that it could crush any obstacle, even if it were a boulder on earth. Once it moved toward me, and I saw that it could crush my bones to powder.

I have been able to see how much power angels have through truths from good from the fact that when angels simply look at them, evil spirits fall down in a faint and no longer look human, and that this lasts until the angel looks away. The reason this sort of thing results from the gaze of angels is that their sight comes from the light of heaven, and heaven's light is divine truth. Eyes correspond to truths from good.

The Language of Angels

ANGELS TALK WITH each other just the way we do in this world. They talk about various things—domestic matters, community concerns, issues of moral life, and issues of spiritual life. There is no difference except that they talk with each other more intelligently than we do because they talk from a deeper level of thought.

I have often been allowed to be in their company and talk with them like one friend with another, or sometimes like one stranger with another; and since at such times I was in a state like theirs, it seemed exactly as though I were talking with people on earth.

Angelic language, like human language, is differentiated into words. It is similarly uttered audibly and heard audibly. Angels have mouths and tongues and ears just as we do; and they also have an atmosphere in which the sound of their language is articulated. However, it is a spiritual atmosphere that is adapted to angels, who are spiritual. Angels breathe in their atmosphere and use their breath to utter words just the way we do in ours.

All people in heaven have the same language. They all understand each other, no matter what community they come from, whether nearby or remote. This language is not learned but is innate; it flows from their very affection and thought. The sound of the language corresponds to their affection and the articulations of the sound—the words, that is—correspond to the mental constructs that arise from their affections. Since their language corresponds to these [inner events], it too is spiritual, for it is audible affection and vocal thinking.

It is recognized that all people have various affections or moods—one in times of happiness, another in times of sorrow, another in times of tenderness and compassion, another in times of honesty and truth, another in times of love and thoughtfulness, another in times of zeal or anger, another in times of pretense and guile, another in times of ambition for respect and adulation, and so on; but there is a dominant affection or love within all of these, so since the wiser angels perceive this, they know from conversation the whole state of another person.

I have been granted knowledge of this through an abundance of experience. I have heard angels discover a person's life simply by listening. They have told me that they know everything about another person's life from a few individual ideas because these enable them to know the person's ruling love, which contains everything in a pattern. This is all that our "book of life" is.

Angelic language has nothing in common with human language except with a few of our words whose sound reflects some feeling, and in this case not with the words themselves but with their sound, which will be further dealt with later.

The fact that angelic language has nothing in common with human language is evidenced by angels' inability to pronounce a single word of a human language. It has been tried, and they could not. The only things they can utter are the ones that are in complete accord with their own affection. Anything that does not agree offends their very life, since their life is a matter of affection and their language flows from it.

I have been told that the first language of people on our earth shared this nature because it was given them from heaven, and that Hebrew resembles it in some respects.

Since angels' language corresponds to the affections of their love, and since heaven's love is love for the Lord and love for our neighbor, we can see how elegant and delightful their conversation is. It affects not only the ears but also the deeper levels of the minds of those who hear it. There was one particular hard-hearted spirit with whom an angel talked, and eventually he was so moved by what the angel was saying that he burst into tears, saying that he couldn't help it, love was talking, and he had never cried before.

The language of angels is also full of wisdom, since it flows from the deeper levels of their thought and their deeper thought is wisdom the way their deeper affection is love. Their love and wisdom unite in speech. As a result, it is so full of wisdom that they can in a single word express what we cannot say in a thousand words; and the concepts of their thinking can encompass things the like of which we cannot grasp, let alone articulate. This is why the things that have been heard and seen in heaven are called inexpressible, such as ear has never heard, nor eye seen.

I have been granted knowledge of this through experience as well. At times I have been conveyed into the state in which angels are and have talked with them in that state. At such times I understood everything, but when I returned to my original state and therefore into the normal thought processes of physical consciousness and wanted to recall what I had heard, I could not. There were a thousand things that would not fit into natural ideas and were therefore inexpressible except by subtle shifts of heavenly light, and not at all, then, in human words.

The same kind of speech we find in the spiritual world is innate in all of us, but in the deeper part of our intellect. However, since for us it does not come down into words that parallel our affections the way it does for angels, we are unaware that we possess it. Yet this is why we have access to the same language as spirits and angels when we arrive in the other life and know how to talk with them without being taught.

There is, as already noted, a single language for everyone in heaven; but it does vary, in that the language of wiser people is more profound and more full of shades of affections and specific concepts. The language of less wise individuals is less profound and not so full, and the language of simple people is still less profound, actually consisting of words that yield meaning only the way they do when we on earth talk with each other.

There is also a language of facial expressions that switch over to a sound modified by ideas, and a language in which images of heaven are combined with concepts and the concepts are presented visually. There is also a language of bodily movements responsive to affections and portraying the same things that their verbal expressions do. There is a language of shared affections and of shared thoughts; there is a thunderous language; and there are other languages as well.

How Angels Talk with Us

ANGELS WHO TALK with us do not talk in their own language but in ours, or in other languages in which we may be fluent—not in languages of which we have no knowledge. The reason for this is that when angels talk with us they turn toward us and unite with us; and one consequence of this union is that the two parties have much the same thought processes. Since our thinking is closely allied with our memory, and our language flows from it, the two parties share the same language. Further, when angels or spirits come to us and unite with us by turning toward us, they enter into our whole memory so completely that it seems exactly as though they themselves know everything we know, including our languages.

The reason angels and spirits are so intimately united to us that it seems to them as though our characteristics were their own is that there is such an intimate union within us of the spiritual and the natural worlds that they are virtually one. However, because we have separated ourselves from heaven, the Lord has provided that there should be angels and spirits with each of us and that we should be governed by the Lord through them. This is the reason there is such an intimate union.

When angels and spirits talk with us, it sounds just as audible as when we talk with each other, but it is not audible to people who are nearby, only to ourselves. This is because the speech of an angel or spirit flows first into our thought and then by an inner route into our organ of hearing so that it activates it from within. Our speech with each other flows first into the air and comes to our organ of hearing and activates it by an outward route. We can see from this that the speech of an angel or spirit with us is heard within us, and that since it activates our hearing mechanism just as much [as our speech with each other does], it is just as audible.

The fact that the speech of an angel or spirit flows down into the ear from within has been made clear to me from the way it flowed into my tongue as well and made it tremble slightly, though not with the actual motion involved when we are articulating the sounds of speech in the formation of words.

Talking with spirits is rarely allowed nowadays, though, because it is dangerous. The spirits then actually know that they are with us, which otherwise they would not; and evil spirits by nature harbor a murderous hatred for us and crave nothing less than our total destruction, body and soul. This is what actually goes on in people who regularly lose themselves in delusions, even to the point that they lose touch with the pleasures appropriate to their natural person.

No angel or spirit is allowed to talk with one of us from the angel's or spirit's own memory, only from that of the individual in question. Angels and spirits actually have memory just as we do. If a spirit were to talk with us from his or her own memory, then it would seem to us entirely as though the thoughts were our own, when they would really belong to the spirit. It is like remembering something that we have never seen or heard. I have been granted knowledge of the truth of this by experience.

This is why some of the ancients were of the opinion that after some thousands of years they would return to their former life and all its deeds, and that they had in fact returned. They gathered this from the fact that sometimes a kind of memory would come up of things that they had never seen or heard. This happened because spirits had flowed from their own memory into the images of these people's thoughts.

Written Materials in Heaven

SINCE ANGELS DO have language and their language is one of words, they also have written materials; and through those written materials just as through their conversation, they express what their minds are sensing. I have sometimes been sent pages covered with writing, just like pages handwritten or printed and published in our world. I could even read them in much the same way, but I was not allowed to get more out of them than a bit of meaning here and there. This was because it is not in keeping with the divine design to be taught by written materials from heaven, but [only] by the Word, since this is the sole means of communication and union between heaven and earth, and therefore between the Lord and humanity.

The occurrence of written materials in the heavens is provided by the Lord for the sake of the Word, for in its essence the Word is the divine truth from which both angels and people on earth get all their wisdom. It has in fact been spoken by the Lord, and what is spoken by the Lord passes through all the heavens in sequence and comes to rest with us. In this way it is adapted both to the wisdom that angels enjoy and to the intelligence that we do. As a result, angels have a Word that they read just as much as we do ours. They draw their doctrinal principles from it, and their sermons come from it. It is the same Word; but its natural meaning, which to us is its literal meaning, does not exist in heaven. There is a spiritual meaning there instead, which is its inner meaning.

Another time I was sent a small page from heaven with only a few words written on it in Hebrew letters. I was told that each letter enfolded treasures of wisdom, and that these were contained in the bends and curves of the letters and therefore in the sounds as well. I could see from this the meaning of the Lord's words, "I tell you in truth, until heaven and earth pass away, not one jot or one tittle shall pass away from the Law" (Matthew 5:18). It is acknowledged in the church that the Word is divine right down to the smallest point, but where in each point the Divine lies hidden—that is not known as yet, so it needs to be explained. In the inmost heaven, the writing consists of various curving and bending forms, and these curves and bends are in keeping with the form of heaven. Through them, angels express the treasures of their wisdom, including many things that they cannot say in words. Believe it or not, the angels know this writing without practice or teachers. They are inwardly gifted with it as they are with the language itself, so this writing is heavenly writing. The reason they are inwardly gifted with it is that all the outreach of angels' thoughts and affections and therefore all communication of their intelligence and wisdom takes place in keeping with heaven's form. This is why their writing flows into that same form.

I have been told that before letters were invented, the earliest humans on our planet had this kind of writing, and that it was transferred into the Hebrew letters, which in early times were all curved, with none marked off by straight lines the way they are now. This is why there are divine things and treasures of heaven in the Word even in its jots and points and little horns.

It is worth knowing that in the heavens, writing flows spontaneously from thoughts. It is done with such ease that it is as though the thought projected itself. The hand does not pause over the choice of some particular word, because the words—both the spoken and the written ones—are responsive to their individual thoughts, and anything that is so responsive is natural and spontaneous.

There are also things written in the heavens without the use of hands, simply in response to thoughts; but these do not last.

I have also seen written materials in heaven comprising nothing but numbers arranged in a pattern and series, just like the writing of letters and words; and I have been told that these writings come from the inmost heaven, whose heavenly writing comes out as numbers for angels in the lower heavens when thought from the higher heaven flows down. I have also been told that this numerical writing enfolds mysteries, some of which cannot be grasped by thought or expressed in words. All numbers do in fact correspond and have meaning depending on their correspondence, just as words do, but with the difference that numbers represent general entities and words specific ones. Since one general entity involves countless specific ones, numeric writing enfolds more mysteries than alphabetic writing does.

I could see from this that numbers in the Word mean things just the way words do. What the simple numbers mean, like 2, 3, 4, 5, 6, 7, 8, 9, 10, and 12, and what the composite ones mean, like 20, 30, 50, 70, 100, 144, 1000, 10,000, and 12,000 and others, may be seen in [my work] *Secrets of Heaven,* where such matters are dealt with.

If people have no concept of heaven and do not want any concept of it other than one of some insubstantial atmosphere in which angels fly around like intellectual minds without the senses of hearing and sight, they cannot believe that angels have language and writing. They locate the entire presence of everything in matter. Yet the things that one finds in heaven occur with just as much reality as those in our world, and the angels who are there have everything they need for life, and everything they need for wisdom.

The Wisdom of Heaven's Angels

WE MAY GATHER how great angels' wisdom is from the fact that in heaven there is a communication that involves everyone. The intelligence and wisdom of one individual is shared with another: heaven is where everyone shares everything of value. This is because the very nature of heavenly love is to want what is one's own to belong to another; so no one in heaven regards his or her good as authentically good unless it is someone else's as well. This is also the basis of heaven's happiness. Angels are led into it by the Lord, whose divine love has this same quality.

I have also been granted knowledge, by experience, of this kind of communication in the heavens. Once some simple people were taken up into heaven, and after they had arrived, they arrived also at an angelic wisdom. They understood things they could not grasp before and said things they could not express in their former state.

Words are not adequate to describe the quality of angels' wisdom—it can be suggested only by some generalizations. Angels can express in a single word what we cannot express in a thousand words. Further, in a single angelic word there are countless things that are beyond the capacity of human words to convey. In the details of angelic speech there are actually treasures of wisdom in unbroken connection, utterly beyond the reach of human knowledge. Then too, what angels cannot evoke with the words of their language they fill in with the sound, which embodies their sensitivity to the proper arrangement of things; for they express their affections through the sounds and the concepts derived from their affections through the words. This is why the things that people have heard in heaven are called ineffable.

Angels can also state completely in a few words the details that are written in a whole volume, giving each word something that raises it toward a deeper wisdom. Their language by nature agrees with their affections, and every word agrees with their concepts. The words actually vary in infinite shadings depending on the way they express in sequence things that are simultaneous in their thought.

The more inward angels can even tell a speaker's whole life from the tone of voice and a few words. From the way the sound is differentiated by concepts into words, they actually perceive the speaker's ruling love, in which, so to speak, the very details of life are engraved.

Angels are constantly being perfected in wisdom, but still they cannot to eternity be so perfected that there is any ratio between their wisdom and the Lord's divine wisdom. For the Lord's divine wisdom is infinite and the angels' is finite, and there is no ratio between the infinite and the finite.

The State of Innocence of Angels in Heaven

NOT MANY PEOPLE in our world know what innocence is or what its quality is, and people involved in evil do not know at all. It is, of course, visible to our eyes—something about the face and the voice and the gestures, especially of infants—but still we do not know what it is, much less that it is where heaven lies concealed within us. To make it known, I should like to proceed in order and talk first about the innocence of infancy, and then about the innocence of wisdom, and finally about the state of heaven in respect to innocence.

The innocence of infancy, or of little ones, is not real innocence, since it is solely a matter of outward form and not internal. Still, we can learn from it what innocence is like, since it does radiate from their faces and from some of their gestures and from their first efforts at speech and affects [the people around them. The reason it is not real innocence is] that they do not have any internal thought—they do not yet know what good and evil are, or what true and false are, and this knowledge is the basis of our thinking. As a result, they do not have any foresight of their own, no premeditation, and therefore no intent of evil. They have no self-image acquired through love for themselves and the world. They do not claim credit for anything, but attribute everything they receive to their parents. They are content with the few little things given them as gifts and enjoy them. They are not anxious about food and clothing or about the future. They do not focus on the world and covet much from it. They love their parents, their nurse, and their little friends and play innocently with them. They are willing to be led, they listen and obey; and since they are in this state, they accept everything as a matter of life. So they have suitable habits, language, and the beginnings of memory and thought without knowing where these gifts come from; and their state of innocence serves as a means of accepting and absorbing them. However, since this innocence is strictly a matter of the body and not of the mind, as already noted, it is external. Their mind is not yet formed, since the mind is our discernment and volition and the thought and affection that come from them.

I have been told from heaven that infants are especially in the Lord's care, and that there is an inflow from the central heaven, where the state is one of innocence, that passes through infants' deeper natures, affecting those natures in its passage only through innocence. This is the source of the innocence they present to our view in their faces and in some of their gestures. It is what deeply affects their parents and creates the love called *storge*.

The innocence of wisdom is real innocence because it is internal, being a property of the mind itself and therefore of our volition itself and our consequent understanding. When there is innocence in these, then there is wisdom as well, because wisdom is a property of volition and understanding. That is why they say in heaven that innocence dwells in wisdom and why angels have as much wisdom as they do innocence. They support the truth of this by observing that people in a state of innocence do not take credit for anything good, but ascribe and attribute everything to the Lord. They want to be led by him and not by themselves, they love everything that is good and delight in everything that is true because they know and perceive that loving what is good—that is, intending and doing good—is loving the Lord, and loving what is true is loving their neighbor. They live content with what they have, whether it is little or much, because they know that they receive as much as is useful—little if little is good for them and much if much is good for them. They do not know what is best for themselves—only the Lord knows; and in his sight everything he supplies is eternal. So they have no anxiety about the future, but refer to anxiety about the future as "care for the morrow," which they say is pain at losing or not getting things that are not needed for their life's useful activities. They never collaborate with friends from evil intent, but only from good, fair, and honest intent. To act from evil intent, they say, is guile, which they avoid like the poison of a snake because it is diametrically opposed to innocence. Since their greatest love is to be led by the Lord, and since they ascribe everything to him, they are kept away from their self-centeredness, and to the extent that they are kept away from their self-centeredness, the Lord flows in. This is why they do not store in their memory what they hear from him, whether through the Word or through preaching, but immediately heed it, that is, intend and do it. Their intention itself is their memory. They appear extraordinarily simple in outward form, but they are wise and provident inwardly. They are the ones the Lord was referring to when he said, "Be wise as serpents and simple as doves" (Matthew 10:16). This is the nature of the innocence called the innocence of wisdom.

Because innocence is the very heart of all the good of heaven, it also affects minds so strongly that people who feel it—which happens at the approach of an angel of the inmost heaven—feel as though they are not under their own control. They are moved by such a joy, so taken out of themselves, so to speak, that it seems as though all the pleasure of the world is nothing by comparison. I speak of this from having experienced it.

All the people in hell are absolutely opposed to innocence. They do not know what innocence is. Their nature is such that the more innocent people are, the more they burn with desire to cause them harm. This is why they cannot stand to see little children. The moment they do, they are consumed with a vicious desire to inflict harm.

The State of Peace in Heaven

ANYONE WHO HAS not experienced heaven's peace cannot know what the peace is that angels enjoy. As long as we are in our bodies, we cannot accept heaven's peace, so we cannot perceive it, our perception being on the natural level. In order to perceive it, we need to be the kind of person who as to thought can be raised and taken out of the body and brought into the spirit so as to be with angels. Since I have perceived heaven's peace in this way, I can describe it, but not in words as it really is, because human words are not adequate. Using words, I can only describe what it is like compared to that peace of mind that people have who are content in God.

There are two things at the heart of heaven, innocence and peace. We say that they are at the heart because they come straight from the Lord. From innocence comes everything good about heaven and from peace comes all the delight of that good. Everything good has its own delight, and both—the good and the delight—are matters of love. This is because what is loved is what is called good and also is perceived as delightful. It follows from this that these two inmost qualities, innocence and peace, emanate from the Lord's divine love and move angels to their very core.

First, we need to say where peace comes from. Divine peace is within the Lord, arising from the oneness of his divine nature and the divine human nature within him. The divine quality of peace in heaven comes from the Lord, arising from his union with heaven's angels, and specifically from the union of the good and the true within each angel. These are the sources of peace. We may therefore conclude that peace in the heavens is the divine nature intimately affecting everything good there with blessedness. So it is the source of all the joy of heaven. In its essence, it is the divine joy of the Lord's divine love, arising from his union with heaven and with every individual there. This joy, perceived by the Lord in the angels and by the angels from the Lord, is peace. It flows down from there to provide angels with everything that is blessed and delightful and happy—what is called "heavenly joy."

Because these are the origins of peace, the Lord is called the Prince of Peace and says that peace comes from him and that peace is in him. So too angels are called angels of peace and heaven the dwelling place of peace, as in the following passages:

A child is born to us, a son is given to us, on whose shoulder the government [shall rest], and his name shall be called Wonderful, Counselor, God, Hero, Eternal Father, Prince of Peace; of the increase of government and peace there shall be no end. (Isaiah 9:5–6 [6–7])

Jesus said, "Peace I leave with you, my peace I give you, not as the world gives do I give to you." (John 14:27)

I have told you these things so that you might have peace in me. (John 16:33)

Because peace means the Lord and heaven and also heavenly joy and the delight of good, greetings in ancient times were—and consequently still are—"Peace be with you." The Lord confirmed this, too, when he sent out his disciples and told them, "When you enter a house, first say 'Peace be upon this house'; and if a child of peace is there, let your peace rest upon it" (Luke 10:5–6). Further, the Lord himself said "Peace be with you" when he appeared to the apostles (John 20:19, 21, 26).

Since divine peace arises from the Lord's union with heaven—and in particular with each individual angel by virtue of the union of the true and the good—when angels are in a state of love they are in a state of peace, because this is when the good within them is united to what is true (angels' states change periodically). Much the same is true of us when we are being regenerated. When a union of the good and the true takes place within us, which happens principally after trials by temptation, we come into a state of delight that arises from heavenly peace.

That peace is like the morning time or dawn in spring, when, once the night has passed, all things of earth begin to take new life from the rising of the sun; the dew that falls from heaven spreads a leafy fragrance far and wide, and springtime's gentle warmth makes meadows fertile and instills its charm in human minds as well. This is because morning or dawn in springtime corresponds to the state of peace of angels in heaven.

The Union of Heaven with the Human Race

THERE ARE GOOD spirits and evil spirits with every individual. We have our union with heaven through the good spirits and our union with hell through the evil ones. These spirits are in the world of spirits.

When these spirits come to us, they come into our whole memory and from there into all our thinking—evil spirits into the matters of memory and thought that are evil, and good spirits into the matters of memory and thought that are good. These spirits are totally unaware that they are with us. Rather, as long as they are, they believe that all these matters of our memory and thought are actually theirs. They do not see us, either, because their sight does not extend to things in our subsolar world.

The Lord takes the greatest care to prevent spirits from knowing whom they are with. If they did know, they would talk with them, and then the evil spirits would destroy them; for evil spirits, being united to hell, want nothing more than to destroy us not only as to spirit (that is, as to our love and faith) but as to our bodies as well. It is different when they do not talk with us. Then they do not know that we are the source of what they are thinking—and what they are saying to each other, since they talk to each other just the way we do—but believe that these matters are their own. They value and love whatever is their own, so these spirits are constrained to love and value us, even though they do not know it.

The reason spirits who are in touch with hell are attached to us as well is that we are born into all kinds of evil, so that our first life is made up of nothing else. Unless spirits of the same kind were associated with us, then, we could not live or be led out of our evils and reformed. So we are kept in our own life by evil spirits and restrained from it by good spirits. Through the two kinds, we are kept in a balance; and since we are in a balance we enjoy an appropriate measure of freedom and can be led out of our evils and turned toward good. This good can be sown in us as well, which could never happen except in our freedom; and the freedom could not be granted us unless spirits from hell were acting on the one side and spirits from heaven on the other, with us in the middle.

I have been shown that to the extent that we exist from our hereditary nature and from ourselves, we could have no life at all if we were not allowed to engage in evil. We would also have no life if we were not in some freedom, and we cannot be compelled to good: anything compelled does not become part of us. I have also been shown that anything good that we accept in freedom is sown in our intentions and becomes virtually our own. This is why we have a communication with hell and a communication with heaven.

The kind of spirit that is associated with us is determined by the kind of person we are in respect to affection and love, though good spirits are assigned to us by the Lord while we ourselves summon the evil ones. The spirits with us change, however, as our own affections change. This means we have one kind with us in infancy, another kind during our childhood, another kind as we are growing up and in early adulthood, and still another kind in old age. During our earliest years, spirits who are in innocence are with us, that is, spirits who are in touch with the heaven of innocence, the inmost or third heaven. In later childhood we are in the company of spirits who are engaged in an affection for knowledge and who are in touch with the ultimate or first heaven. As we are growing up, during our early adulthood, spirits who are responsive to affections for what is true and good and therefore with intelligence are with us. They are spirits who are in touch with the second or intermediate heaven. In old age, though, spirits who are in wisdom and innocence are with us, spirits therefore who are in touch with the inmost or third heaven.

Still, this association is arranged by the Lord for people who can be reformed and regenerated. It is different for people who cannot be reformed or regenerated. Good spirits are assigned to them as well in order to restrain them from evil as much as possible, but their direct connection is with the evil spirits who are in touch with hell. This means that the spirits are of the same nature as the people they are associated with. Whether they love themselves or money or revenge or adultery, the same kind of spirits are with them and are, so to speak, taking up residence in their evil affections. To the extent that we cannot be restrained from evil by good spirits, they inflame us, and to the extent that an evil affection is in control, they cling to us and will not back off.

In this way, evil people are united to hell and good people to heaven.

I have talked with angels about the union of heaven with the human race and have told them that church people actually do say that everything good is from the Lord and that there are angels with us, but few people really believe that angels are so close to us, much less that they are in our thought and affection. The angels have told me that they knew this kind of [empty] belief and talk occurred in the world, and especially (which astonished them) in the church, where people have the Word that teaches them about heaven and its union with them. Yet in fact the union is so vital that we could not think the least thought apart from the spirits who are with us. Our spiritual life depends on this. They said that the reason for this ignorance was that people believe they live on their own, without any connection with the Ultimate Reality of life, and do not know that there is this connection through the heavens. Yet if that connection were severed, we would instantly drop down dead. If we believed the way things really are, that everything good comes from the Lord and everything evil from hell, then we would not take credit for the good within us or blame for the evil. Whenever we thought or did anything good, we would focus on the Lord, and any evil that flowed in we would throw back into the hell it came from.

Heaven's Union with Us through the Word

WE HAVE BEEN so created that we have a connection and a union with the Lord, while with angels we have only an association. The reason we have only an association, not a union, with angels is that we are from creation like angels in respect to the deeper levels of our minds. We have a similar purposefulness and a similar capacity to understand. This is why we become angels after death if we have lived according to the divine pattern, and why we then, like the angels, have wisdom. So when we talk about our union with heaven, we mean our union with the Lord and our association with angels, since heaven is not heaven because of anything that really belongs to the angels but because of the divine nature of the Lord.

Over and above what angels have, though, there is the fact that we are not just in a spiritual world by virtue of our inner natures but are at the same time in a natural world by virtue of our outward natures. These outward things that are in the natural world are all the contents of our natural or outer memory and the thinking and imaging we do on that basis. In general, this includes our insights and information together with their delights and charm to the extent that they have a worldly flavor, and all the pleasures that derive from our physical senses. Then too, there are those senses themselves and our words and actions. All these are ultimate things in which the Lord's divine inflow comes to rest, since it does not stop in the middle but goes on to its very limit.

We may gather from this that the ultimate form of the divine pattern is in us, and since it is the ultimate form, it is the basis and foundation.

Since the Lord's divine inflow does not stop in the middle but goes on to its very limit, as just stated, and since the intermediate region it crosses is the angelic heaven and the limit is in us, and since nothing disconnected can exist, it follows that there is such a connection and union of heaven with the human race that neither can endure without the other. If the human race were cut off from heaven, it would be like a chain with a link removed, and heaven without the human race would be like a house without a foundation.

However, since we have broken this connection by turning our inward natures away from heaven and toward the world and ourselves through our self-love and love of the world and have so pulled away that we no longer serve heaven as its basis and foundation, the Lord has provided a medium to serve in place of that basis and foundation and to maintain the union of heaven with humanity. That medium is the Word.

I have been told from heaven that the earliest people had direct revelation because their inner natures were turned toward heaven, and that this was the source of the Lord's union with the human race at that time. After those times, though, there was not the same kind of direct revelation, but an indirect revelation through correspondences. All their divine worship consisted of these; so the churches of those times were called symbolic churches. They knew what correspondences and representations were and that everything on earth answered to spiritual things in heaven and the church (or represented them, which amounts to the same thing). In this way, the natural elements that constituted their outward worship served them as means for thinking spiritually and therefore thinking with angels.

Once all knowledge of correspondences and representations had been lost, then a Word was written in which all the words and the meanings of the words are correspondences and therefore contain that spiritual or inner meaning in which angels are engaged.

So when we read the Word and grasp it in its literal or outward meaning, angels grasp it in its inner or spiritual meaning. In fact, all the thought of angels is spiritual, while ours is natural. These two kinds of thought do seem different, but they are one because they correspond.

I have talked with angels about the Word on occasion, and have told them that it is looked down on by some people because of its pedestrian style. They know absolutely nothing about its deeper meaning and therefore do not believe that this kind of wisdom lies hidden within. The angels have told me that even though the style of the Word may appear pedestrian in its literal meaning, it is qualitatively incomparable because divine wisdom lies hidden not just in the overall meaning but in every word, and that this wisdom shines out in heaven.

Heaven and Hell Come from the Human Race

PEOPLE IN THE Christian world are totally unaware that heaven and hell come from the human race. They actually believe that angels were created in the beginning and constitute heaven, and that the devil or Satan was an angel of light who became rebellious and was cast out together with his faction, and that this gave rise to hell.

Angels are utterly amazed that there can be this kind of belief in the Christian world, and even more so that people know absolutely nothing about heaven, even though this is a primary doctrine of the church. Knowing that this kind of ignorance is prevalent, they are profoundly delighted that it has now pleased the Lord to reveal to us so much about heaven—and about hell as well—and so as much as possible to dispel the darkness that is rising daily because this church is drawing to a close. So they want me to testify on their behalf that in all heaven there is not a single angel who was created as such in the beginning, nor is there in all hell a devil who was created as an angel of light and cast out. Rather, all the people in heaven and in hell are from the human race—in heaven the ones who have lived in heavenly love and faith, and in hell the ones who have lived in hellish love and faith.

There are people who say, "Who has come back from heaven and told us that it exists, or from hell, to say that it exists? What is this business about people being tortured by fire to eternity? What is this Judgment Day? Haven't we been waiting for it for centuries, all in vain?" along with any number of other things that imply a denial of everything. Many people who are particularly skilled in worldly affairs think like this; so to prevent them from further disturbing and misleading people of simple faith and simple heart and bringing on a hellish darkness concerning God, heaven, eternal life, and the other matters that follow from them, the deeper reaches of my spirit have been opened by the Lord, enabling me to talk after their death with all the people I have ever known during their physical lives. I have talked with some for days, with some for months, and with some for a year.

Many people who have just died, when they have discovered that they are living persons just as they were before, and in a similar state (for our first state after death is like the one we were in on earth, although this changes gradually for us either toward heaven or toward hell), have been moved by a newfound joy at still being alive. They have said they would not have believed it. They were absolutely amazed that they had been in such ignorance and blindness about the state of life after death.

Many of the scholars of the Christian world are dumbfounded when they find themselves after death in bodies, wearing clothes, and in houses the way they were in this world. When they call to mind what they had thought about life after death, the soul, spirits, and heaven and hell, they are embarrassed and say that they had been thinking nonsense. They say that people of simple faith had been far wiser than they.

Non-Christians, or People Outside the Church, in Heaven

THE GENERAL OPINION is that people who have been born outside the church, the people called "the nations" or "non-Christians," cannot be saved because they do not have the Word and therefore do not know the Lord; and without the Lord there is no salvation. They could know, however, that these people too are saved simply from the fact that the Lord's mercy is universal, that is, it is extended to all individuals. Non-Christians are born just as human as people within the church, who are in fact few by comparison. It is not their fault that they do not know the Lord. So anyone who thinks from any enlightened reason at all can see that no one is born for hell. The Lord is actually love itself, and his love is an intent to save everyone. So he provides that everyone shall have some religion, an acknowledgment of the Divine Being through that religion, and an inner life. That is, living according to one's religious principles is an inner life, for then we focus on the Divine; and to the extent that we do focus on the Divine, we do not focus on the world but move away from the world and therefore from a worldly life, which is an outward life.

People can realize that non-Christians as well as Christians are saved if they know what constitutes heaven in us. The heaven within us is our acknowledgment of the Divine and our being led by the Divine. The beginning and foundation of every religion is its acknowledgment of the Divine Being; a religion that does not acknowledge the Divine Being is not a religion at all. The precepts of every religion focus on worship, that is, on how the Divine is to be honored so that we will be acceptable in its sight; and when this fully occupies the mind (or, to the extent that we intend this or love this) we are being led by the Lord.

The heaven in one individual is not the same as the heaven in another. It differs in each according to the affection for what is good and true. If people are absorbed in an affection for what is good for the sake of the Divine, they love divine truth because the good and the true love each other and want to be united. Consequently, non-Christian people who have not had access to genuine truths in the world still accept them in the other life because of their love.

There was one spirit from a non-Christian country who had lived a good and thoughtful life according to his religion in this world. When he heard some Christian spirits discussing their creeds (spirits talking to each other reason much more exhaustively and acutely than people on earth, especially about what is good and true), he was astonished to find that they quarreled. He said he did not want to listen, since they were arguing on the basis of deceptive appearances. His advice to them was, "If I am a good person, I can know what is true simply from its goodness, and I can be open to what I do not know."

There are wise and simple people among non-Christians just as there are among the Christians. To show me what they were like, I have been allowed to talk with both kinds, sometimes for hours and even for days. Nowadays, though, there are not wise ones like those of ancient times, especially in the early church (this covered much of the Near East and was the source from which religion spread to many non-Christian peoples). I have been allowed to carry on personal conversations with some of them in order to find out what they were like.

One particular individual was with me who had been one of the wise at one time and who was therefore well known in the scholarly world. I talked with him about various subjects and was given to believe that he was Cicero. Since I knew that he was wise, we talked about wisdom, intelligence, the pattern of reality, the Word, and finally about the Lord. On wisdom, he said that there was no wisdom that was not a matter of life, and that wisdom could not be an attribute of anything else. On intelligence, he said that it came from wisdom. On the pattern of reality, he said that the pattern comes from the Supreme Deity, and that living in accord with this pattern is being wise and intelligent. As to the Word, when I read him something from the prophets he was utterly enchanted, especially at the fact that the individual names and individual words referred to deeper realities. He was quite astonished that modern scholars take no pleasure in this pursuit. I could sense very clearly that the deeper levels of his thought or mind were open. He said that he could not remain present because he felt something too holy for him to bear, it affected him so deeply.

It often happens that when non-Christians come into the other life, if they have worshiped some god in the form of an image or statue or idol, they are introduced to people who take on the roles of those gods or idols in order to help rid them of their illusions. After they have been with these people for a few days, they are taken away.

If they have worshiped particular individuals, then they are introduced either to those people themselves or to individuals who play their parts. Many Jews, for example, are introduced to Abraham, Jacob, Moses, or David; but when they realize that they are just as human as anyone else and that they have nothing special to offer them, they are embarrassed, and are taken off to whatever place is in keeping with their lives.

Of non-Christians, the Africans are especially valued in heaven. They accept the good and true things of heaven more readily than others do. They want especially to be called obedient, but not faithful. They say that Christians could be called "faithful," since they have a doctrine of faith, but only if they accept the doctrine—or, as the Africans say, if they can accept it.

The Lord's church is spread throughout the whole world. It is universal, then, and consists of all individuals who have lived in the virtue of thoughtfulness according to the principles of their religions. In relation to the people outside it, the church where the Word is and the Lord is known through it is like the heart and lungs of the human body, which give life to all the organs and members of the body according to their forms, locations, and connections.

Children in Heaven

SOME PEOPLE BELIEVE that only children born in the church get into heaven, not children born outside the church. They say this is because children born in the church are baptized and are introduced into the faith of the church by this baptism. They do not realize that no one gets either heaven or faith by baptism. Baptism serves only as a sign and reminder that we need to be reborn, and that people born in the church can be reborn because the Word is there, the Word that contains the divine truths that make regeneration possible. The church is where the Lord, who is the source of rebirth, is known.

May it be known, therefore, that every child who dies, no matter where he or she was born, within the church or outside it, of devout or irreverent parents, is accepted by the Lord after death, brought up in heaven, taught according to the divine design and filled with affections for what is good and through them with direct knowledge of the truth; and then, being continually perfected in intelligence and wisdom, all such individuals are led into heaven and become angels.

Anyone who thinks rationally can realize that no one is born for hell—everyone is born for heaven. We ourselves are to blame if we arrive in hell, but children are not yet liable for any blame.

Children who die are still children in the other life. They have the same kind of childlike mind, the same innocence in their ignorance, the same total delicateness—they are only in the rudiments of becoming angels; for children are not angels in being but only angels in becoming. Actually everyone who leaves this world stays in the same state of life—a baby is in the state of a baby, a child in the state of a child, an adolescent or adult or senior in the state of an adolescent, an adult, or a senior. However, this state eventually changes. A child's state is better than the others, though, in regard to innocence, and in regard to the fact that children have not yet let evils take root in them by actually living them. The quality of innocence is such that everything heavenly can be sown in it, because innocence is the vessel of the truths of faith and the good affections of love.

The condition of children in the other life is vastly better than that of children in our world because they are not clothed with an earthly body. Instead, they have an angelic one. An earthly body is inherently heavy. It does not receive its primary sensations and primary impulses from the inner or spiritual world but from the outer or natural one; so children in this world learn by practice to walk, to do things, and to talk—even their senses, such as sight and hearing, are developed by use. It is different for children in the other life. Because they are spirits, their actions are impelled directly by their inner natures. They walk without practice and even talk, though at first this is just a matter of general affections as yet undifferentiated into mental concepts. However, they are very soon introduced into these latter as well, since their outer natures are in such concord with their inner natures. Then too, angels' speech flows from their affections, varied by the concepts of their thought, so that their speech is in perfect agreement with the thoughts that arise from their affections.

As soon as children are reawakened (which happens immediately after their death), they are taken to heaven and given to female angels who had loved children tenderly during their physical lives and had loved God as well. Since in this world they had loved all children with a kind of maternal tenderness, they accept these new ones as their own, and the children love them as their mothers as though this were inborn in them. Each such angel has as many children as her spiritual maternal nature wants.

We need to explain briefly how children are brought up in heaven. They learn to talk from their nurse. Their first speech is only the sound of their affection, which gradually becomes more articulated to the extent that the concepts they are thinking enter in, since such concepts arising from affections make up the whole angelic language.

The first things instilled into these affections (which all stem from their innocence) are the kinds of thing they see with their eyes that particularly delight them; and since these are from a spiritual origin, aspects of heaven flow into them that serve to open their deeper natures. In this way they become more perfect every day. Once this first age has been completed, they are taken to another heaven where they are taught by instructors, and so on.

I have also been shown how all these things are instilled using delightful and charming means that are suited to their natures. I have in fact been allowed to see children clothed most becomingly, with garlands of flowers around their chests glowing with the most charming and heavenly colors, and similar ones around their slender arms. Once I was even allowed to see some children with their nurses, in the company of some young women in a paradisal garden—not a garden of trees, but one with vaulted arches of something like laurels making the most intricate doorways with paths offering access inward—and the children themselves dressed with like beauty. When they entered, the flowers over the entrance radiated the most joyous light imaginable. This enabled me to gather what their delights were like and how they were led into the blessings of innocence and thoughtfulness by things charming and delightful, with the Lord constantly instilling blessings by means of these charming and delightful gifts.

By a means of communication that is common in the other life, I have been shown what children's concepts are like when they are looking at various objects. It is as though everything were alive; so in the smallest concepts of their thought there is an inherent life. I gathered that children on earth have concepts that are much the same when they are involved in their play, for they do not yet have the kind of reflective thought that grownups have about what is inanimate.

Many people think that children remain children in heaven and are like children among the angels. People who do not know what an angel is can corroborate this opinion because of the images here and there in churches, where angels are represented as children. However, things are actually very different. Intelligence and wisdom make an angel, qualities that they do not have as long as they are children. Children are with the angels, but they themselves are not angels yet. Once they are intelligent and wise they are angels for the first time. In fact—something that has surprised me—then they no longer look like children but like adults, because they no longer have a childlike nature but a more grown-up angelic nature. This goes with intelligence and wisdom.

The reason children look more grown-up as they are perfected in intelligence and wisdom—that is, like adolescents and young adults—is that intelligence and wisdom are the essential spiritual food. So the things that nourish their minds also nourish their bodies, which is a result of correspondence, since the form of the body is nothing but an outward form of their inner natures.

It does need to be known that children in heaven do not grow up beyond the prime of youth, but remain at that age forever. To assure me of this, I have been allowed to talk with some who had been raised as children in heaven and had grown up there, with some while they were still children, and then later with the same ones when they had become youths; and I have heard from them about the course of their life from one age level to another.

I have talked with angels about children, wondering whether they were free from evils because they did not have any realized evil the way adults do. I was told, though, that they are equally involved in evil, even to the point that they too are nothing but evil. However, they, like all angels, are withheld from their evils by the Lord and kept focused on what is good to the point that it seems to them as though they were focused on what is good of their own accord. So to prevent children from having a false notion about themselves after they have grown up in heaven—a belief that the good that surrounds them is from them and not from the Lord—they are let back into their hereditary evils from time to time and left in them until they know and recognize and believe the way things really are.

There was one individual who had died in infancy and grown up in heaven who had this kind of opinion. He was the son of a particular king; so he was let back into his own innate life of evil. I could tell then from the aura of his life that he had a drive to lord it over others and regarded adultery as of no concern whatever— evils that were part of his heredity from his parents. Once he recognized that he was like this, though, he was again accepted among the angels he had been with before.

Rich and Poor People in Heaven

THERE ARE VARIOUS opinions about acceptance into heaven. Some people think that the poor are accepted but not the rich; some think that rich and poor alike are accepted; some think that rich people cannot be accepted unless they give up their assets and become like the poor—and all of them support their opinions from the Word. However, as far as heaven is concerned, people who differentiate between the rich and the poor do not understand the Word. At heart, the Word is spiritual, though it is natural in the letter; so if people take the Word only in its literal meaning and not in some spiritual meaning they go astray in all kinds of ways, especially regarding the rich and the poor. They believe that it is as hard for rich people to enter heaven as it is for a camel to go through the eye of a needle and that it is easy for the poor by reason of their poverty, since it says, "Blessed are the poor, because theirs is the kingdom of the heavens" (Luke 6:20–21).

However, people who know something about the spiritual meaning of the Word think differently. They know that heaven is for everyone who lives a life of faith and love, whether rich or poor. We will explain below who are meant by "the rich" in the Word and by "the poor."

Out of a great deal of conversation and living with angels, I have been granted sure knowledge that rich people enter heaven just as easily as poor people do, and that no one is shut out of heaven for having abundant possessions or accepted into heaven because of poverty. There are both rich and poor people there, and many of the rich are in greater splendor and happiness than the poor.

By way of preface, we may note that it is all right to acquire wealth and accumulate any amount of assets, as long as it is not done by fraud or evil devices. It is all right to eat and drink with elegance, as long as we do not invest our lives in such things. It is all right to be housed as graciously as befits one's station, to chat with others like ourselves, to go to games, to consult about worldly affairs. There is no need to walk around looking pious with a sad, tearful face and a bowed head. We can be happy and cheerful.

I have talked after their death with some people who during their earthly lives had renounced the world and devoted themselves to a virtually solitary life, wanting to make time for devout meditation by withdrawing their thoughts from worldly matters. They believed that this was the way to follow the path to heaven. In the other life, though they are gloomy in spirit. They avoid others who are not like themselves and they resent the fact that they are not allotted more happiness than others. They believe they deserve it and do not care about other people, and they avoid the responsibilities of thoughtful behavior that are the means to union with heaven. They covet heaven more than others do; but when they are brought up to where the angels are, they cause anxieties that upset the happiness of angels. So they part company; and once they have parted, they betake themselves to lonely places where they lead the same kind of life they had led in the world.

Many people who devoted their energies to business and trade in the world, many who became rich, are in heaven. There are not so many, though, who made a name for themselves and became rich in public office. This is because these latter were led into love for themselves and the world by the profits and the positions they were given because of their administration of justice and morality and of profits and positions. This in turn led them to deflect their thoughts and affections from heaven and direct them toward themselves; for to the extent that we love ourselves and the world and focus on ourselves and the world exclusively, we estrange ourselves from the Divine and move away from heaven.

What awaits rich people who do not believe in the Divine Being and reject matters of heaven and the church from their minds is hell, where they find filth and wretchedness and want. When wealth is loved as an end, it turns into things like these, and not only the wealth itself but also what it is used for—the pampered living, the indulgence in pleasures, the wider and freer dedication to amorality, the self-exaltation over people they belittle. Because these riches and these functions have nothing spiritual in them, only earthly qualities, they turn to filth.

Poor people do not get into heaven because of their poverty but because of their lives. Our lives follow us whether we are rich or poor. There is no special mercy for the one any more than for the other. People who have lived well are accepted; people who have lived badly are rejected.

Poverty can actually seduce people and lead them away from heaven just as much as wealth can. There are many people among the poor who are not content with their lot, who covet much more, and who believe that wealth is a blessing; so when they do not get what they want, they are enraged and harbor evil thoughts about divine providence. They envy other people in their assets, and given the chance would just as soon cheat them and live in their own foul pleasures.

It is different, though, for poor people who are content with their lot, are conscientious and careful in their work, prefer work to idleness, behave honestly and reliably, and lead Christian lives.

We may gather from this that rich people arrive in heaven just as much as poor people do, one as easily as the other. The reason people believe that it is easy for the poor and hard for the rich is that the Word is misunderstood when it talks about the rich and the poor. In the spiritual meaning of the Word, "the rich" means people who are amply supplied with understandings of what is true and good, that is, people in the church where the Word is. "The poor" means people who lack these understandings, but who long for them, or people outside the church, where the Word is not found.

We need also to explain who are meant by the rich of whom the Lord said, "It is easier for a camel to go through the eye of a needle than for a rich person to enter the kingdom of God" (Matthew 19:24). "The rich person" here means the rich in both senses, natural and spiritual. Rich people in the natural sense are people who have abundant wealth and set their hearts on it, while in a spiritual sense they are people who are amply supplied with insights and knowledge (for these are spiritual wealth) and who want to use them to get themselves into heavenly and ecclesiastical circles by their own intellect. Since this is contrary to the divine design, it says that it is easier for a camel to get through the eye of the needle. On this level of meaning, a camel means our cognitive and informational level in general, and the eye of a needle means spiritual truth.

Marriages in Heaven

SINCE HEAVEN COMES from the human race, which means that there are angels of both sexes there, and since by creation itself woman is for man and man for woman, each for the other, and since this love is inborn in both sexes, it follows that there are marriages in the heavens just as there are on earth. However, the marriages in the heavens are very different from earthly ones.

Marriage love finds its source in the union of two people in one mind. In heaven, this is called "living together," and they are not called "two" but "one." Consequently two spouses in heaven are not called two angels but one angel.

The reason for this kind of union of husband and wife on the deepest levels of their minds goes back to creation itself. The male is born to focus on cognitive processes, and therefore bases his thinking on his intellect. In contrast, the woman is born to focus on intentions, and therefore bases her thinking on her own volition. We can see this from the tendency or innate nature of each as well as from their form. As to innate nature, men do act on the basis of reason, while women act on the basis of their feelings. As to form, the man

125

has a rougher and less attractive face, a deeper voice, and a stronger body, while the woman has a softer and more attractive face, a gentler voice, and a softer body. This is like the difference between intellect and volition or between thought and affection.

Genuine marriage love is not possible between one husband and more than one wife. Polygamy in fact destroys the spiritual source of marriage love, whose purpose is to form one mind out of two. It therefore destroys the deeper union of the good and the true that is the very essence of that love. Marriage with more than one is like an intellect divided among more than one will or like a person pledged to more than one church. This actually pulls faith apart so that it becomes no faith at all.

Few people do experience true marriage love, and if people are not intent on this, they have absolutely no knowledge of the inner delight that dwells within that love. They are aware only of the delight of lust, a delight that turns disagreeable after people have lived together for a little while. The delight of real marriage love, though, not only lasts into old age on earth but even becomes heavenly delight after death, when it is filled with a deeper delight that becomes better and better to eternity.

The angels even said that the blessings of real marriage love could be listed in the thousands, with not a single one known to people here or comprehensible to the understanding of anyone who is not in a marriage of the good and the true from the Lord.

Any love of control of one over the other utterly destroys marriage love and its heavenly pleasure, for as already noted, marriage love and its pleasure consist of the intent of one belonging to the other, and of this being mutual and reciprocal. A love of being in control in a marriage destroys this because the dominant partner simply wants his or her will to be in the other, and does not want to accept any element of the will of the other in return. So it is not mutual, which means that there is no sharing of any love and its pleasure with the other, and no accepting in return. Yet this sharing and the union that follows from it is the very inward pleasure that is called blessedness in marriage. Love of being in control stifles this blessedness, and with it absolutely everything heavenly and spiritual about the love, to the point that even all knowledge of its existence is lost. One could even say that it is held so cheaply that the mere mention of [marriage] blessedness makes people laugh or flare up in anger.

When one partner wants or loves what the other does, then there is a freedom for both, because all freedom stems from love. However, there is freedom for neither one when there is control. One is the servant; and so is the one in control, because he or she is being driven like a servant by a need to be in control.

Between partners who are in marriage love there are heavenly pleasures almost like games of innocence to their minds, like those of babies, because there is nothing that does not delight them. Heaven flows into the smallest details of their lives with its joy. This is why marriage love is pictured in heaven by the loveliest things of all. I have seen it represented by an indescribably lovely young woman enveloped by a white cloud. I was told that all the beauty of angels in heaven comes from marriage love. The affections and thoughts that flow from it are represented by gleaming auras, like those of fiery gems or rubies, all this accompanied by feelings of delight that move the deeper levels of the mind.

In a word, heaven portrays itself in marriage love because heaven for angels is the union of the good and the true, and it is this union that constitutes marriage love.

Marriages in the heavens differ from marriages on earth in that earthly marriages are also for the purpose of having children, while this is not the case in the heavens. In place of the procreation of children there is the procreation of what is good and true. The reason for this replacement is that their marriage is a marriage of the good and the true, as presented above, and in this marriage what is good and true is loved above all, as is their union; so these are what are propagated by the marriages in the heavens. This is why in the Word births and generations mean spiritual births and generations, births of what is good and true. The mother and father mean the true united to the good that is prolific, the sons and daughters the good and true things that are born, and the sons-in-law and daughters-in-law mean the unions of these [descendants], and so on.

We can see from this that marriages in the heavens are not the same as marriages on earth. In the heavens there are spiritual weddings that should not be called weddings but unions of minds, because of the union of the good and the true. On earth, though, there are weddings, because they concern not only the spirit but the flesh as well. Further, since there are no weddings in the heavens, two spouses there are not called husband and wife, but because of the angelic concept of the union of two minds into one, each spouse is identified by a word that means "belonging to each other."

I have also been allowed to see how marriages are entered into in the heavens. Throughout heaven, people who are similar gather together and people who are dissimilar part company. This means that every community consists of like-minded people. Like are drawn toward like not by their own will but by the Lord. In the same way, spouse is drawn toward spouse when their minds can be united into one. So at first sight they love each other most deeply, see each other as married partners, and enter into their marriage. This is why all of heaven's marriages are the work of the Lord alone. They also hold a feast in celebration with many people gathered; these feasts differ from community to community

I could tell that everyone in hell is opposed to marriage love from the aura that emanated from hell. It was like a ceaseless effort to break up and destroy marriages.

I have been shown how the pleasures of marriage love lead to heaven and how the pleasures of adultery lead to hell. The path of marriage love toward heaven led into constantly increasing blessings and delights until they were beyond number or description. The deeper they were, the more of them there were and the more indescribable they were, all the way to the delights of the inmost heaven, the heaven of innocence. All this was accomplished with the greatest freedom, because all freedom stems from love; so the greatest freedom comes from marriage love, which is the essential heavenly love. On the other hand, the path of adultery led toward hell, step by step to the very lowest where there is nothing that is not grim and terrifying. This is the kind of fate that awaits adulterers after their life in the world. By "adulterers," we mean people who find pleasure in acts of adultery and not in marriage.

What Angels Do in Heaven

THERE IS NO way to list all the functions that people have in the heavens or to describe them in detail, though it is possible to say something on the subject in general terms; they are innumerable and vary depending on the roles of the communities as well. In fact, each community plays a unique role, since the communities differ depending on their virtues and therefore on their function. This is because virtues for everyone in the heavens are virtues in act, which are functions. Everyone there does something specifically useful, for the Lord's kingdom is a kingdom of uses.

There are many services in the heavens just as there are on earth, since there are ecclesiastical, civic, and domestic affairs there. The existence of the ecclesiastical ones follows from what was presented about divine worship, the existence of civic ones from what was presented about forms of government in heaven, while the existence of domestic ones follows from the material on angels' homes and houses and on marriages in heaven. We can therefore see that the roles and services in any given heavenly community are multiple.

All the communities in the heavens are differentiated according to their forms of service because they are differentiated according to their virtues. Their virtues are virtues in action or acts of thoughtfulness, which are services. There are some communities whose tasks are to take care of babies; there are other communities whose tasks are to teach and lead children while they are growing up; there are other communities that look after young boys and girls who are well disposed because of the way they were raised in this world and have come [straight] to heaven, where they are taught and raised in much the same way. There are some that teach simple people from the Christian world and lead them on the way to heaven, and there are some that do the same for various non-Christian peoples. There are some that protect new spirits, just arrived from the world, from the attacks of evil spirits; and there are some who attend to people in the lower earth. Then there are some who attend to people in the hells and control them so that they do not torture each other beyond set limits. There are also some who tend to people who are being awakened from their death.

Broadly speaking, angels of all communities are assigned to us to protect us, to lead us away from evil feelings and the evil thoughts that these cause and to instill good feelings to the extent that we are freely open to them. These serve to control our deeds or works by removing our evil intentions to the extent that this can be done. When angels are with us they seem to dwell in our affections, near us to the extent that we are engaged in something good because of truth, and distant to the extent that our life is removed from such engagement.

However, all these tasks are things the Lord does by means of angels, since angels do them not on their own but from the Lord. This is why in the deeper meaning of the Word "angels" does not mean angels but something of the Lord; and this is why angels are called gods in the Word.

These are general categories of angels' activities, but each individual has her or his own specific contribution to make. This is because every general service is made up of countless elements that are called mediate or subservient or supporting services. All of these are arranged and ranked according to the divine design, and taken together they make up and complete an overarching function that is the common good.

The people in heaven who are involved in church affairs are the ones who loved the Word in the world and looked for truths in it with lively interest, not for the sake of eminence or profit but for the service of their own life and the lives of others. In proportion to their love and eagerness for service, they are enlightened there and are in the light of wisdom, attaining it because of the Word in the heavens, which is not natural the way it is in the world, but spiritual. They have the gift of preaching; and in keeping with the divine design, the ones who are more highly placed there are the ones who surpass others in the wisdom they derive from their enlightenment.

The people who are involved in civic affairs are the ones who loved their country and its welfare more than their own, who behaved honestly and fairly out of a love for what is honest and fair. To the extent that they sought out laws of justice because of the urging of this love and thereby became discerning they enjoy the ability to fill governing offices in heaven. They perform these duties in the place or on the level appropriate to their discernment, which in turn is equivalent to their love of service in the common good.

Further, there are so many offices and departments in heaven, so many tasks, that there are simply too many to list. There are relatively few in the world. No matter how many people are involved, they are all caught up in a love of their work and tasks out of a love of service—no one out of selfishness or a love of profit. In fact, there is no love of profit for the sake of livelihood, since all the necessities of life are given them gratis. They are housed gratis, clothed gratis, and fed gratis. We can see from this that people who have loved themselves and the world more than service have no place in heaven. In fact, our love or affection invariably stays with us after our life in the world. It is not uprooted to eternity.

Everyone in heaven is engaged in his or her work according to its correspondence, and the correspondence is not with the work itself but with the use of each particular task; and everything has a correspondence. When we are engaged in an activity or a task in heaven that does answer to its use, then we are in a state of life very much like the one we were in in this world. This is because what is spiritual and what is natural act as one by means of their correspondence, but with the difference that [after death] we enjoy a deeper delight because we are engaged in a spiritual life. This is a deeper life, and therefore more open to heavenly blessedness.

Heavenly Joy and Happiness

HARDLY ANYONE NOWADAYS knows what heaven is or what heavenly joy is. People who think about either subject come up with such pedestrian and crude notions that they scarcely amount to anything at all. I have had a wonderful opportunity to learn from spirits who were coming from this world into the other life what kind of idea they had about heaven and heavenly joy, for when they are left on their own, as they were in the world, they still think the same way.

The reason they do not know about heavenly joy is that people who think about it at all base their judgments on the external joys of the natural person. They do not know what the inner or spiritual person is, so they do not know what that person's pleasure and blessedness are. So even if they were told by people involved in spiritual or inner joy what heavenly joy is and how it feels, they would not be able to grasp it.

Everyone is capable of knowing that when we leave our outer or natural person we enter our inner or spiritual one; so we can also know that heavenly pleasure is an inner and spiritual pleasure and not an outer or natural one. Since it is inner and spiritual, it is purer and finer and moves our deeper levels, the levels of our soul or spirit.

We may also conclude from this that the quality of our pleasure follows from the quality of the pleasure of our spirit, and that the pleasures of our bodies, called "the pleasures of the flesh," have nothing to do with heaven by comparison. Whatever is in our spirit when we leave the body remains with us after death, for we then live as human spirits.

By its very nature, heaven is full of pleasures, even to the point that if we see it as it really is, it is nothing but bliss and pleasure. This is because the divine good that emanates from the Lord's divine love constitutes heaven both overall and in detail for everyone there; and divine love is the intent that everyone should be saved and should be most profoundly and fully happy. This is why it is all the same whether you say "heaven" or "heavenly joy."

Heaven's pleasures are both indescribable and innumerable; but no one can realize or believe anything about their multitude who is wholly wrapped up in pleasures of the body or the flesh. This, as I have already said, is because their deeper levels are looking away from heaven toward the world, which is backward. For no one who is wholly involved in pleasures of the body or the flesh (or in love for oneself and the world, which is the same thing) feels any pleasure except in eminence or profit or in physical and sensory gratification. These stifle and smother deeper pleasures of heaven so completely that people do not even believe such pleasures exist. So they would be quite bewildered if they were so much as told that any pleasures remain once the pleasures of eminence and profit have been taken away; and they would be even more bewildered if they were told that the pleasures that take their place are countless and simply defy comparison with pleasures of the body and the flesh, especially pleasures of eminence and profit. We can see, then, why people do not know what heavenly joy is.

We may gather the magnitude of heaven's pleasure simply from the fact that for everyone there it is delightful to share their pleasure and bliss with someone else; and since everyone in the heavens is like this, we can see how immense heaven's pleasure is. For there is in heaven a sharing by everyone with each individual, and by each individual with everyone.

This kind of sharing flows from the two loves of heaven, which are love for the Lord and love for our neighbor. These loves by nature want to share their pleasures. The reason love for the Lord is like this is that because the Lord's love is a love of sharing everything it has with everyone, it intends the happiness of everyone. Much the same love exists in individuals who love him, because the Lord is in them. So there is a mutual sharing of angels' pleasures with each other. We shall see later that love for our neighbor is like this as well. We may gather from all this that these loves by nature want to share their pleasures.

The faint sense of pleasure, the almost imperceptible sense of well-being that was found in people who were focused on love for God and love for their neighbor in the world, turns into the pleasure of heaven, perceptible and palpable in countless ways. That sense of well-being that had been lying hidden in their deeper natures while they lived in the world is now unveiled and released into open sensation, because now they are in the spirit, and this was the delight of their spirit.

All the pleasures of heaven are united to forms of service and dwell within them, because forms of service are the good effects of the love and thoughtfulness that angels are immersed in. Consequently, the nature of each individual's pleasures depends on the nature of that individual's service, and its intensity depends on the intensity of the affection for service.

These pleasures are inherent in the senses because of the inflow of heaven, where all pleasure belongs to service and depends on service.

On the basis of an opinion formed in the world, some spirits have believed that heavenly happiness consisted of a life of leisure, being waited on by others; but they were informed that there is never any happiness in idling around in order to be content. This would mean wanting the happiness of others for oneself, in which case no one would have any at all. This kind of life would be idle, not active, a life that would lead to atrophy. They might in fact have known that apart from an active life, a life has no happiness, and that idleness serves that life only for refreshment, in order to return them to the active life with more energy. Then they were shown in many ways that angelic life consists of worthwhile, thoughtful actions, actions that are useful to others, and that all the happiness angels have is found in service, derives from service, and is proportional to service.

So that these people might feel shame (people who have had the notion that heavenly joy consists of a life of leisure, inhaling eternal bliss) they are enabled to perceive what kind of life this would be. They see that it is thoroughly miserable; and once all their delight therefore dies away, they are very soon disgusted and nauseated.

Almost all the people who arrive in the other life think that hell is the same for everyone and that heaven is the same for everyone, when in fact there are infinite variations and differences in each. Hell is never the same for any two people, nor is heaven. In the same way, no one of us, no spirit, and no angel is ever exactly like any other, even facially. When I even thought about two identical or equal beings, the angels were aghast. They said that every unity is formed by a harmonious agreement of many constituents and that the nature of the unity depends on the nature of the agreement. This is how every community of heaven forms a unity and how all the communities form a single heaven, which is accomplished solely by the Lord, by means of love.

Useful activities in the heavens occur in similar variety and diversity. The function of one individual is never exactly the same as that of any other, so the delight of one is never the same as another's. Not only that, the delights of each function are countless, and these countless delights are equally varied, yet they are united in a design that enables them to focus on each other as do the functions of the individual members and organs and viscera in the human body; or even more, like the functions of every vessel and fiber in those members and organs and viscera. These are all interconnected in such a way that they focus on what they can contribute to the other and therefore to all, with all mindful of the individual members. They act as one because of this regard for the whole and for the individual.

Some wondered whether there was that kind of love in heaven, whether it was possible for anyone to love her or his neighbor more than herself or himself. They were told, though, that in the other life everything good increases immensely. Life in a physical body cannot by nature progress beyond loving one's neighbor as the self, because it is immersed in physical concerns. Once these are removed, though, the love becomes purer and ultimately angelic, which is loving one's neighbor more than oneself. This is because in the heavens doing good for someone else is a delight and doing good for oneself is not unless it is to give to another and therefore for the sake of the other. This is loving one's neighbor more than oneself.

As for the possibility of this love, it was said that in this world it might be gathered from the marriage love some people have for each other, people who would rather die than allow their spouse to be hurt. Or they might consider the love of parents for their children, the mother who would rather starve than see her children go hungry; or the true friendship that leads people to face peril for the sake of their friends.

Heaven does not consist of wanting to be least in order to be greatest. People who do this pant and long for greatness. Rather, it means a heartfelt wishing better for others than for oneself, and serving others for the sake of their happiness with no thought of reward, simply out of love.

Actual heavenly joy as it is in and of itself is beyond description because it dwells in the deepest natures of angels. It flows from there into the details of their thought and affection and from these into the details of their speech and action. It is as though their deeper levels were wide open and freed to accept a delight and bliss that spreads out through all their fibers and therefore through their whole being, giving them a kind of perception and feeling that simply cannot be described.

Some spirits wanted to know what heavenly joy was, so they were allowed to feel it to the point that they could not bear any more. Still, this was not angelic joy, but only the slightest trace of the angelic quality that they were allowed to observe and share. It was so slight that it was almost cool, yet they called it most heavenly because it was so deep within them. I could tell from this not only that there are levels of heavenly joy, but also that the deepest level

139

of one individual barely touches the outmost or some median level of another. I could also see that when we do reach our own deepest level we are in our own heavenly joy and that we could not bear anything deeper because it would become painful for us.

To enable me to know what heaven and heavenly joy are and what their quality is, though, the Lord has allowed me to feel the pleasures of heavenly joy often and at length. Because this was living experience, I may indeed know about them, but there is no way to describe them. Still, something should be said in order to provide at least some notion about them. There is an effect of countless pleasures and joys that unite to present a single something, a unity or united affection that contains a harmony of countless affections that do not come through to consciousness individually, only vaguely, because the consciousness is so very general. It was still possible to perceive that there were countless elements within it, so beautifully arranged as to defy description. The qualities of those countless elements flow from the very design of heaven; and this kind of design is resident in the very least affections, affections that are manifest and perceived only as a very general unity, depending on the perceptive ability of the subject.

I have also noticed that heavenly joy and delight seemed to be coming from my heart, spreading very subtly through all my inner fibers and from there into the gatherings of fibers with such a profound sense of pleasure that my fibers seemed to be nothing but joy and delight, and everything I perceived and felt was alive with bliss. Next to these joys, the joy of physical pleasures is like crude and irritating dust compared to a pure and gentle breeze.

I noticed that when I wanted to convey all my pleasure to someone else, a deeper and fuller pleasure flowed in ceaselessly in its place. The more I wanted to convey it, the more it flowed in; and I perceived that this was from the Lord.

People in heaven are continually progressing toward the springtime of life. The more thousands of years they live, the more pleasant and happy is their springtime. This continues forever, increasing according to the growth and level of their love, thoughtfulness, and faith.

As the years pass, elderly women who have died of old age—women who have lived in faith in the Lord, thoughtfulness toward their neighbor, and in contented marriage love with their husbands—come more and more into the flower of growing youth and into a beauty that surpasses any notion of beauty accessible to our sight. Their goodness and thoughtfulness is what gives them their form and gives them its own likeness, making the pleasure and beauty of thoughtfulness radiate from every least corner of their faces so that they become actual forms of thoughtfulness. Some people have seen them and have been stunned. The form of thoughtfulness that is open to view in heaven is like this because it is thoughtfulness itself that both gives and is given visible form. In fact, it does this in such a way that the whole angel, especially her face, is virtually thoughtfulness itself appearing to open perception. When people look at this form, its beauty is unutterable, affecting the very inmost life of the mind with thoughtfulness. In a word, to grow old in heaven is to grow young. People who have lived in love for the Lord and in thoughtfulness toward their neighbor are forms like this, or beauties like this, in the other life. All angels are forms like this, in infinite variety. This is what makes heaven.

The Vastness of Heaven

THE VASTNESS OF the Lord's heaven follows from many of the things that have been presented above, especially from the fact that heaven is from the human race, not only that portion of it born within the church but also the portion born outside it. This means that heaven includes everyone who has lived a good life since the very beginning of our planet.

Anyone familiar with the continents and regions and nations of this world may gather what a multitude of people there are on our whole globe. Anyone who goes into the mathematics of it will discover that thousands and thousands of people die on any given day, making hundreds of thousands or millions every year; and this has been going on since the earliest times, thousands of years ago. All of these people have arrived in the other world, called the spiritual world, after their decease, and they are still arriving.

I cannot say how many of these are or are becoming angels of heaven. I have been told that most of the earliest people became angels, because they thought more deeply and spiritually and were therefore enveloped in heavenly affection; while for later ages it was not so many because as time passed we became more externally minded and began to think more on the natural level, which meant that we were enveloped in more earthly affection.

This enables us to gather at the outset that heaven is huge simply from the inhabitants of this planet.

Then too, I have talked with spirits about the fact that people could realize that there is more than one earth in the universe from the fact that the starry heaven is so immense. There are so incomprehensibly many stars in it, each one a sun in its own place and its own system, like our sun, of different magnitudes. If people think this through carefully, they will come to the conclusion that this whole vast universe cannot be anything but a means to an end, which is the goal of creation, a heavenly kingdom in which the Divine can dwell with angels and with us. The visible universe, the heaven spangled with so incomprehensibly many stars that are all suns, is in fact simply a means for the production of planets with people on them who can make up a heavenly kingdom.

Given all this, rational people cannot help thinking that such a vast means toward such an end did not come into being for the sake of a human race on one earth. What would that be for a divine being, an infinite being, for whom thousands or tens of thousands of planets, all fully inhabited, would be so slight as to be practically nothing?

By a preliminary calculation, if there were a million planets in the universe with three hundred million people on each one, and two hundred generations over six thousand years, and if each person or spirit were allotted three cubic cubits, and if all these people or spirits were gathered into one place, they would not even fill the volume of our earth, hardly more than a satellite of one of the planets. This would be such a small space in the universe as to be barely visible, since we can scarcely see those satellites with the naked eye. What would this be for the Creator of the universe, for whom it would not be enough if the whole universe were filled? For the Creator is infinite.

I have talked about this with angels, who have told me that they have much the same idea about how small the number of the human race is in comparison to the infinity of the Creator. However, they do not think in terms of space but of states, and to their minds, no matter how many tens of thousands of planets you could conceive of, it would still be simply nothing to the Lord.

Because they take a few passages from the Word literally, some people think that heaven is not vast but small. For example, there are places where it says that only the poor will be accepted into heaven, or only the elect, or only people in the church and not people from outside, or only people for whom the Lord makes intercession, or that heaven will be closed when it is full, and that the time for this is foreordained. These people do not realize that heaven will never be closed; that there is no foreordained time, no fixed number; and that "the elect" are people who live lives of goodness and truth; that "the poor" are people who have not found out what is good and true but who long to (they are also called "the hungry" because of this longing).

People who think that heaven is small because they have misunderstood the Word can only be thinking that heaven is in a single place where everyone is gathered together. Yet in fact heaven consists of countless communities. Further, they can only be thinking that heaven is granted to individuals out of direct mercy and therefore consists simply of admission and acceptance out of good will. They do not realize that the Lord, out of his mercy, leads everyone who accepts him, and that the people who accept him are the people who live according to the laws of the divine design, which are precepts of love and faith. They do not realize that being led by the Lord from infancy to the end of earthly life and then on to eternity is what mercy really means. If only they knew that everyone is born for heaven, that people are accepted into heaven who accept heaven into themselves in this world, and that people who do not accept it are shut out! ☀

Part 3

HELL

The Lord Governs the Hells

IN THE EARLIER discussion of heaven, it was made clear throughout that the Lord is the God of heaven and that the whole government of the heavens is in the Lord's hands. Since the relationship of heaven to hell and of hell to heaven is like that of two opposites that act against each other, with the action and reaction yielding the state of equilibrium within which everything exists, in order for absolutely everything to be kept in this balance, it is necessary that the ruler of the one be the ruler of the other as well. That is, unless the same Lord controlled the attacks of the hells and restrained their madness, the balance would be destroyed; and if the balance were destroyed, everything else would go.

I have sometimes been allowed to sense the aura of malevolent falsity flowing out of hell. It was like a constant effort to destroy everything good and true, united to an anger, a kind of rage at not being able to do so. Especially, it was an effort to destroy the divine nature of the Lord because this is the source of everything good and true.

I have sensed an aura of benevolent truth from heaven, though, that served to restrain the rage of the effort rising up from hell, which yielded an equilibrium. I perceived that the sole source of this aura was the Lord, even though it seemed to be coming from angels in heaven. The reason it comes solely from the Lord and not from angels is that every angel in heaven admits that nothing of what is good and true comes from herself or himself, but that it all comes from the Lord.

I need to explain briefly how the hells are governed, though. Overall, the hells are governed by a general impingement of divine good and divine truth from the heavens through which the general effort that flows out of the hells is restrained and controlled. There is also a specific impingement from each heaven and from each community of heaven.

Specifically, the hells are governed by means of angels who are given the ability to look into the hells and check the insanities and riots there. Sometimes angels are sent there, and their very presence brings matters under control.

In general, though, all the people in the hells are governed by their fears, some by fears sown and still in place from the world. However, since these fears are not adequate and gradually weaken, they are governed through fears of punishment, which are the primary means of preventing them from doing evil. There are many kinds of punishment there, milder or more severe depending on the evil [they are restraining]. Most of the time, the relatively malevolent spirits are in power, having gained control by their experience and skill; and they are able to keep the rest in servile obedience by punishments and the fears that these give birth to. These dominant spirits do not dare go beyond fixed limits.

We do need to realize that the only way of controlling the violent rages of people in the hells is through fear of punishment. There are no other means.

The Lord Does Not Cast Anyone into Hell:
Spirits Cast Themselves In

SOME PEOPLE CHERISH the notion that God turns his face away from people, spurns them, and casts them into hell, and is angry against them because of their evil. Some people even go so far as to think that God punishes people and does them harm. They support this notion from the literal meaning of the Word where things like this are said, not realizing that the spiritual meaning of the Word, which makes sense of the letter, is wholly different. So the real doctrine of the church, which is from the spiritual meaning of the Word, teaches something else. It teaches that the Lord never turns his face away from anyone or spurns anyone, never casts anyone into hell or is angry.

Anyone whose mind is enlightened perceives this while reading the Word simply from the fact that the Lord is goodness itself, love itself, and mercy itself. Good itself cannot do harm to anyone. Love itself and mercy itself cannot spurn anyone, because this is contrary to mercy and love and is therefore contrary to the divine nature itself. So people who are thinking with an enlightened mind when they read the Word perceive clearly that God never turns away from us, and that because he does not turn away from us, he behaves toward us out of goodness and love and mercy. That is, he wills well toward us, loves us, and has compassion on us.

We can gather from this that we do evil from hell and good from the Lord. However, since we believe that whatever we do comes from ourselves, the evil we do clings to us as though it were our own. This is why we are at fault for our evil, never the Lord. The evil within us is hell within us, for it makes no difference whether you say "evil" or "hell." Since we are at fault for our evil, it is we, not the Lord, who lead ourselves into hell. Far from leading us into hell, the Lord frees us from hell to the extent that we do not intend and love to be absorbed in our evil. Our whole volition and love stays with us after death. People who have intended and loved what is evil in the world intend and love what is evil in the other life, and then they no longer allow themselves to be led away from it. This is why people who are absorbed in evil are connected to hell and actually are there in spirit; and after death they crave above all to be where their evil is. So after death, it is we, not the Lord, who cast ourselves into hell.

I need to mention how this happens. When we arrive in the other life, we are first taken up by angels who do everything for us and also tell us about the Lord, heaven, and angelic life and offer us lessons in what is good and true. However, if we as spirits are the kind of people who have been familiar with things like this in the world but have denied or rejected them at heart, then after some conversation we want to get away from them and try to leave. When the angels notice this, they leave us. After spending some time with various other people, we eventually take up with people who are devoted to similar evils. When this happens, we are turning away from the Lord and turning our faces toward the hell we were united to in the world, where people live who are engaged in a similar love of evil.

We can see from this that the Lord is leading every spirit toward himself through angels and through an inflow from heaven, but that spirits who are absorbed in evil resist strenuously and virtually tear themselves away from the Lord. They are drawn by their evil—by hell, that is, as though it were a rope; and because they are drawn and want to follow because of their love of evil, it follows that they freely cast themselves into hell.

This is hard to believe in the world because of people's notions about hell. In fact, it does not even look that way in the other life.

Evil spirits are punished severely in the world of spirits to keep them terrified of doing evil. This too seems to come from the Lord, but still no punishment there does come from the Lord. It comes from the evil itself, since an evil is so closely united to its punishment that they cannot be separated. The hellish mob craves and loves nothing more than inflicting harm, especially punishing and torturing, and they do inflict harm and punishment on anyone who is not being protected by the Lord. So when something evil is being done from an evil heart, since this rejects any protection by the Lord, evil spirits assail the evildoer and inflict punishment.

To some extent, this can be illustrated by evil deeds and their punishments in the world, where they are also united. The laws here set penalties for each crime, so anyone who plunges into evil is plunging into its punishment as well. The only difference is that in the world, evil can be hidden, which cannot happen in the other life.

We can therefore conclude that the Lord does not do harm to anyone. It is like this in the world as well. It is not the king or the judge or the law that is responsible for the punishment of the guilty, because they are not responsible for the evil of the criminal.

All the People Who Are in the Hells
Are Absorbed in Evils and Consequent Falsities
because of Their Loves of Themselves and the World

SEEN IN ANY of heaven's light, all the spirits in the hells appear in the form of their own evil. Each one is in fact an image of her or his evil, since for each individual the inner and outer natures are acting as a unit, with the deeper elements presenting themselves to view in the outer ones—in the face, the body, the speech, and the behavior. So you can tell what they are like by looking at them. In general, they are forms of contempt for others, threats against people who do not revere them; they are forms of various shadings of hatred, of various forms of vengefulness. Savagery and cruelty show through from within.

It does need to be known, though, that hellish spirits look like this in heaven's light, but that they look human to each other. This is a gift of the Lord's mercy, so that they do not look as repulsive to each other as they do to angels. However, this appearance is deceiving, since the moment a ray of light from heaven is let in, these human forms turn into the monstrous ones that they are essentially, the forms just described, because in heaven's light everything appears as it really is. This is also why they avoid heaven's light and dive into their own illumination, an illumination like that of glowing coals or, in places, like burning sulfur. This light, though, turns into pure darkness when any ray of light from heaven flows in. This is why the hells are described as being in gloom and darkness, and why the gloom and darkness mean the kinds of malevolent distortions characteristic of hell.

At first I wondered why love for oneself and love of the world are so diabolic, why people who are absorbed in them look so frightful. After all, in the world we scarcely give love for ourselves a second thought. We focus only on that outward inflation of spirit called pride, which we believe is the only self-love because it is so visible. Not only that, if love for oneself does not express itself in pride, then we in the world think it is the vital fire that rouses us to work for high position and to do constructive things. We believe that if we saw no prospect of esteem and glory in these efforts, our spirits would become sluggish. People ask, "Who would do anything decent or useful or remarkable except to be praised and respected by others, [openly] or in their thoughts; and where does this come from except from the fire of a love for glory and esteem— that is, for the sake of self?" This is why people in the world do not realize that in its own right love for oneself is the love that rules in hell and that makes hell within us.

Since this is in fact the case, I should like first to describe what love for oneself is, and then explain that everything evil and false wells up from this love.

Love for oneself is intending well to oneself alone, not to others except for the sake of oneself—not the church, the country, or any human community. It is helping them solely for the sake of one's own reputation and rank and glory. Unless these can be seen in the services we offer, we are saying at heart, "What difference does it make? Why should I? What's in it for me?" So we forget it. We can see from this that people who are absorbed in a love for themselves do not love their church or country or community or any constructive activity. They love only themselves. Their only pleasure lies in self-gratification; and since the pleasure that stems from love constitutes human life, their life is a life of self. A life of self is a life that depends on what we claim as our own, and in its own right what we claim as our own is nothing but evil.

People who love themselves do love their own as well, their own being specifically their children and grandchildren and more broadly all who ally with them, whom they call "their own people." Loving both the former and the latter is actually loving themselves, because they regard the others as though they were in themselves, and focus on themselves in others. These "others" who are claimed as their own include everyone who praises and reveres and worships them.

We are completely absorbed in our self-image and therefore in our hereditary evil whenever we focus on ourselves in anything worthwhile we are doing, for we are focusing on ourselves and away from what is good and not on what is good and away from ourselves. So in the worthwhile activities we set up an image of ourselves and not an image of the Divine. I have been assured of this by experience as well. There are evil spirits who live halfway between the north and the west, underneath the heavens, who are particularly skilled at getting upright spirits involved in their self-image and therefore focused on various kinds of evil. They do this by getting them absorbed in thinking about themselves, either openly by words of praise and esteem or covertly by focusing their feelings exclusively on themselves. To the extent that they succeed, they turn the faces of the upright people away from heaven and also becloud their understanding, calling up evils from their self-concern.

If you look at their origins and essences, you can see that love for oneself and love of one's neighbor are opposites. In people who are wrapped up in love for themselves, love of their neighbor begins from self. They claim that everyone is her or his own neighbor; and from this as a center they reach out to all who ally with them, with progressively less intensity depending on the love that unites the others with them. They regard people outside this group as worthless, and people who offer opposition to them and their evildoing they regard as enemies. It does not matter what they are actually like, whether they are wise or upright or honest or fair.

Picture a community made up of people like this, all totally in love with themselves, not caring about others unless they are allies, and you will see that their love is no different from that of thieves for each other. To the extent that they are acting in concert, they embrace each other and call each other friends; but once they stop cooperating, once anyone resists their control, they attack and butcher each other. If their deeper natures—their minds—are probed, it will be clear that they are full of virulent hatred for each other, that at heart they ridicule anything fair and honest and even ridicule the Deity, tossing it aside as worthless. This comes out even more clearly from their communities in the hells, which will be described below.

In broad terms, the evils characteristic of people focused on love for themselves are contempt for others; envy; enmity toward anyone who is not on their side, and a consequent hostility; various kinds of hatred; vengefulness; craft; deceit; callousness; and cruelty. In religious matters, this extends not only to a contempt for the

Divine and for the divine gifts that are the true and good elements of the church; it extends also to anger at such things, an anger that turns into hatred when we become spirits. Then not only can we not stand hearing about these matters, we blaze with hatred against everyone who acknowledges and worships the Divine.

As for love of the world, it is not so intensely opposed to heavenly love, because there are not so many evils latent in it.

Love of the world is wanting to divert the wealth of others to ourselves by any means available. It is setting our heart on wealth and allowing the world to distract us from the spiritual love that is love for our neighbor and therefore from heaven and the Divine.

This love takes many forms, though. We may love wealth in order to be raised to exalted rank simply because we love exalted rank. We may love exalted rank and high position for the sake of wealth. We may love wealth for the sake of the various pleasures it offers in the world. We may love wealth simply for the sake of wealth, which is avarice, and so on. The purpose of being wealthy is called its use, and purpose or use is what gives a love its quality. That is, the quality of a love is determined by the goal it aims at. Everything else serves it as means.

Hellfire and Gnashing of Teeth

UNTIL NOW, HARDLY anyone has known the meaning of the eternal fire and gnashing of teeth ascribed to people in hell in the Word. This is because people think materialistically about statements in the Word, in ignorance of its spiritual meaning. So some of them understand the fire to be material fire, some think it is torment in general, some the pangs of conscience, some that it is just words meant to strike a terror of evil into us. Some understand the gnashing of teeth to be a kind of grinding, some only the kind of shudder we feel when we hear this kind of clash of teeth.

Anyone familiar with the spiritual meaning of the Word, though, can realize what eternal fire and gnashing of teeth are, since there is spiritual meaning in every expression and in the meaning of every expression in the Word. At heart, that is, the Word is spiritual, and spiritual meaning can be expressed to us only in natural terms because we are in a natural world and think on the basis of what we encounter in it.

For us human beings, spiritual warmth is the warmth of life, because as already noted it is essentially love. This love is what fire means in the Word. Heavenly fire means love for the Lord and love for our neighbor, and hellish fire means love for ourselves and love of the world.

Hellish fire or love has the same source as heavenly fire or love, namely heaven's sun or the Lord. However, it is changed into hellfire by the people who receive it, for all inflow from the spiritual world varies depending on how it is received or depending on the forms into which it flows. The same thing happens with the warmth and light from the world's sun. Warmth flowing from this source into woods and flower beds produces vegetation and pleasant, soft aromas. The same warmth flowing into manure or carrion produces decay and foul stenches. Similarly, light from the same sun on one object produces lovely, charming colors, while on another it produces ugly and unpleasant ones. It is the same with the warmth and light from heaven's sun, which is love. When that warmth or love flows into good recipients, like good people and spirits or angels, it makes their goodness fertile; whereas when it flows into evil people it has the opposite effect. Their evils either stifle it or distort it. Similarly, when heaven's light flows into the true perceptions of good will, it yields intelligence and wisdom; but when it flows into malicious distortions, it changes there into insanity and various kinds of illusion. Everything depends on reception.

It does need to be known, though, that the people in the hells are not actually in fire. The fire is an appearance. They do not actually feel any burning, only the kind of warmth they knew in the world. The reason there seems to be fire is correspondence, since love corresponds to fire, and everything we see in the spiritual world has its visible form from its correspondence.

The gnashing of teeth, though, is the constant clash and strife of false convictions with each other (and therefore the warfare of the individuals who hold the false convictions) united to contempt for others, hostility, derision, mockery, and blasphemy. These even break out into various kinds of butchery. Everyone there is defending his or her own false convictions and calling them true. From outside the hells, these clashes and battles sound like gnashing teeth, and they turn into the gnashing of teeth when truths from heaven flow into hell.

In these hells dwell all the people who acknowledged nature and denied the Divine. The people who deliberately convinced themselves are in the deeper hells. Since they cannot accept any ray of light from heaven and can therefore not see anything within themselves, most of them focus on their senses and their bodies. These are people who do not believe anything they cannot see with their eyes and touch with their hands. So for them, all sensory illusions are the truths on which they base their arguments. This is why their arguments sound like the gnashing of teeth. It is because in the spiritual world all false statements grate, and teeth correspond to the outmost aspects of nature and to our own outmost natures, which have to do with our senses and our bodies.

The Malice and Unspeakable Skills of Hellish Spirits

ANYONE WHO THINKS deeply and knows anything about the workings of the human mind can see and understand how significantly superior spirits are to other people. In a minute, we can consider and turn over and decide in our minds more than we can express in speech or writing in half an hour. This shows how much better we are when we are in the spirit and therefore when we become spirits, since it is the spirit that thinks and the body is what the spirit uses to express its thoughts in speech or writing.

This is why people who become angels after death have access to indescribable intelligence and wisdom relative to the intelligence and wisdom they had while they were living in the world. While they were living in the world, their spirits were confined in a body and by that means were in the natural world. So when the spirit did think spiritually, the thoughts flowed into natural concepts that are relatively general, crude, and hazy. This means they are not open to the countless elements characteristic of spiritual thought. They also immerse them in the thickets of the cares of the world. It is different once the spirit has been freed from the body and has arrived at its own spiritual state, which happens when it crosses from the natural world to the spiritual world that is appropriate to it.

The level of wisdom and intelligence for angels is also the level of malice and craft among hellish spirits. The issue is much the same because once the human spirit is freed from its body it devotes itself wholly to its virtue or to its vice. An angelic spirit devotes itself to its virtue and a hellish spirit to its vice. This means that just as angelic spirits think and intend and speak and act from their good, so hellish spirits do the same from their evil. It was different while they were living in the flesh because then the evil of their spirits was under the restraints that apply to all because of the law, or because of money, position, reputation, and their fears of losing these things. So the evil of their spirits could not break out and show itself in its true colors. Further, the evil of their spirit then lurked hidden by veils of outward integrity, honesty, fairness, and affection for what is true and good, qualities that such people presented and simulated in their speech for worldly reasons. All the while, the evil remained so hidden and veiled that they themselves scarcely knew that there was so much malice and craft in their spirits, that they were therefore intrinsically the very devils they would become after death when their spirits would come into their own and display their own nature.

The kind of malice that surfaces then defies all belief. There are thousands of things that burst forth from the evil itself then, including some that are beyond the words of any language to describe. I have been allowed to learn and even to observe what they are like by many experiences because the Lord has granted me to be in the spiritual world as to my spirit while I was in the natural world as to my body. This I can testify: their malice is so great that scarcely a thousandth part of it can be described. Further, if the Lord did not protect us we would never be able to escape from hell; for with each of us there are both spirits from hell and angels from heaven. Further, the Lord cannot protect us unless we acknowledge the Divine and live faithful, thoughtful lives. Otherwise, we are turning away from the Lord and toward hellish spirits and are therefore in spirit absorbing the same kind of malice. Still, the Lord is constantly leading us away from the evils that we assimilate and attract by associating with these spirits, leading us if not by the inner restraints of conscience (which we do not accept if we deny the Divine), then by the outer restraints already listed, the fears of the laws and their penalties, of the loss of money and the forfeiture of rank and reputation. People like this can be led away from evils through the delights of their love and the fear of losing and forfeiting these delights, but they cannot be led into spiritual virtues. To the extent that they are led into them, you see, they convert them into guile and craft by pretending to be good and honest and fair-minded with a view to persuading and deceiving others. This guile is added to the evil of their spirits and gives it form, lending its own nature to the evil.

The Appearance, Location, and Number of the Hells

IN THE SPIRITUAL world, the world where spirits and angels live, things look much the same as they do in the natural world where we live—so similar that at first glance there seems to be no difference. You see plains there, mountains, hills, and cliffs with valleys between them, you see bodies of water and many other things that we find on earth. However, they all come from a spiritual source, so they are visible to the eyes of spirits and angels but not to our eyes because we are in a natural world. Spiritual people see things that come from a spiritual source, and natural people see things that come from a natural source. This means that there is no way for our eyes to see things in the spiritual world unless we are allowed to be in the spirit, or until we become spirits after death. On the other hand, angels and spirits are utterly incapable of seeing anything in the natural world unless they are with some one of us who has been allowed to talk with them. Our eyes are adapted to receive the light of the natural world, and the eyes of angels and spirits are adapted to receive the light of the spiritual world; yet the two kinds of eyes look exactly alike.

Natural people cannot understand that the spiritual world is like this, and sense-centered people even less so, being people who believe nothing unless they can see it with their physical eyes and touch it with their hands. This means they believe only what they glean through their sight and touch and that they think on this basis; so their thought is material and not spiritual.

Because of this resemblance between the spiritual world and the natural world, it is hard for people after death to realize that they are not in the world where they were born, the world they have just left; so they actually call death nothing but a crossing from one world into another like it.

The hells are not visible [to angels in the heavens and spirits in the world of spirits] because they are closed. All one can see are the entrances, called gates, when they open to admit spirits like the ones already there. All the gates into the hells open from the world of spirits, none from heaven.

There are hells everywhere. They are under the mountains and hills and cliffs and under the plains and valleys. The openings or gates to the hells that are under the mountains and hills and cliffs look at first sight like crevices or fissures in the rocks. Some of them are quite broad and open, some narrow and confined, full of rough places. All of them seem dim and gloomy when you look in, although the hellish spirits who live there have the kind of illumination you get from glowing coals. Their eyes are adjusted to the reception of this kind of light. This is because when they were living in the world they were in darkness about divine truths owing to their denial of them. They were in a kind of light as to their false convictions because they affirmed them, which gave their eyesight the form it has. This is also why heaven's light is darkness to them, so when they come out of their caves, they cannot see anything. This makes it abundantly clear that we come into heaven's light to the extent that we have acknowledged the Divine and affirmed within ourselves the values of heaven and the church. We come into the darkness of hell to the extent that we have denied the Divine and affirmed within ourselves values contrary to those of heaven and the church.

I have been allowed to look into the hells and see what they were like inside, for when it pleases the Lord, a spirit or angel who is overhead can probe visually into the depths and examine their nature with no coverings in the way. I have also been allowed to explore them in this fashion. Some of the hells looked to me like caves and caverns leading into cliffs and then slanting downward or off at an angle.

Some of these hells looked like the lairs or dens of wild animals in the woods, some like the vaulted chambers and crypts found in mines, with caverns leading downward. Many of the hells are three-fold. The higher ones look gloomy inside because the people there are fond of malicious distortions. The lower ones look fiery, though, because their inhabitants are devoted to malice itself. Darkness in fact corresponds to malicious distortions, and fire to the actual malice. That is, the people in the deeper hells are the ones who acted from evil on a deeper level, while the people in the hells that are not so deep acted from evils on a more superficial level—that is, on the basis of their malicious distortions.

In some hells you can see what look like the ruins of houses and cities after a fire, where hellish spirits live and hide out.

In the milder hells you can see crude huts, sometimes grouped in something like a city, with alleyways and streets. There are hellish spirits in these homes, with constant quarrels, hostility, beating, and violence. The streets and alleys are full of thieves and robbers.

In some hells there are nothing but brothels, foul to look at and full of all kinds of filth and excrement.

There are also dark forests where hellish spirits roam like wild beasts; and there are underground caves there where they flee when they are being threatened by others. Then there are desert areas where everything is barren and sandy, with rugged cliffs here and there with caves in them, and huts scattered around as well. People are exiled from the hells into these desert places if they have suffered to the limit, especially people who in the world were craftier than others in the skills of deliberate manipulation and deceit. This kind of life is their final lot.

There is an infinite variety to everything evil just as there is to everything good. People do not grasp this if they have only simplistic concepts of particular evils like contempt, hostility, hatred, vengefulness, deceit, and the like; but they should realize that each of these contains so many distinctive forms, each of which also contains distinctive or particular forms, that a whole volume would not be adequate to list them. The hells are so clearly arranged according to the distinctive features of everyone's evil that nothing could be more definitely and clearly arranged. We can gather from this that they are beyond counting, some near each other and some far removed according to the general, specific, and particular differences of their evils.

The Equilibrium between Heaven and Hell

THERE IS A constant balance between heaven and hell. An effort to do evil is constantly emanating upward from hell, and an effort to do good is constantly emanating down from heaven. The world of spirits is in this equilibrium.

The reason the world of spirits is in this equilibrium is that after death we first enter the world of spirits and are kept in the same state we were in in the world. This could not happen unless there were a perfect balance there. This allows everyone to be examined there as to quality, since we keep the same kind of freedom we had in the world. Spiritual equilibrium is a state of freedom for us and for spirits.

Everything in the heavens and the hells is so arranged that each individual there is in a personal equilibrium. We can to some extent gather this from what has already been presented concerning the heavens and the hells. That is, all the communities of heaven are very precisely differentiated according to the genera and species of their goodness, and all the communities of hell according to the genera and species of their evils. Further, there is a corresponding community of hell underneath every community of heaven, and this opposing correspondence yields an equilibrium. So the Lord is constantly making sure that the hellish community under any heavenly one does not get too strong. To the extent that one begins to get too strong, it is brought under control by various means and returned to its proper balanced relationship. I shall mention only a few of the many means. Some involve a stronger presence of the Lord. Some involve closer communication and union of one or more communities with others. Some involve the exile of extra hellish spirits into desert places, some the transfer from one hell to another, some the reorganization of the people in the hells, which also is accomplished in various ways. Some involve concealing some of the hells under thicker and heavier coverings, some sending them down deeper. Then there are other means, some involving the heavens overhead.

I mention this so that there may be some grasp of the fact that only the Lord provides that there shall be a balance between good and evil everywhere, and therefore between heaven and hell. On this kind of equilibrium depends the salvation of everyone in the heavens and everyone on earth.

～

WHAT I HAVE been saying in this book about heaven, the world of spirits, and hell will be obscure to people who find no delight in knowing about spiritual truths; but it will be clear to people who do have this delight, especially to people involved in an affection for truth for its own sake—that is, people who love truth because it is true. Anything that is loved enters into the concepts of our minds with light, especially when what is loved is true, because all truth is in the light. ✳

About Emanuel Swedenborg

EMANUEL SWEDENBORG (1688–1772) was born Emanuel Swedberg (or Svedberg) in Stockholm, Sweden, on January 29, 1688 (Julian calendar). He was the third of the nine children of Jesper Swedberg (1653–1735) and Sara Behm (1666–1696). At the age of eight he lost his mother. After the death of his only older brother ten days later, he became the oldest living son. In 1697 his father married Sara Bergia (1666–1720), who developed great affection for Emanuel and left him a significant inheritance. His father, a Lutheran clergyman, later became a celebrated and controversial bishop, whose diocese included the Swedish churches in Pennsylvania and in London, England.

After studying at the University of Uppsala (1699–1709), Emanuel journeyed to England, Holland, France, and Germany (1710–1715) to study and work with leading scientists in western Europe. Upon his return he apprenticed as an engineer under the brilliant Swedish inventor Christopher Polhem (1661–1751). He gained favor with Sweden's King Charles XII (1682–1718), who gave him a salaried position as an overseer of Sweden's mining industry (1716–1747). Although he was engaged, he never married.

After the death of Charles XII, Emanuel was ennobled by Queen Ulrika Eleonora (1688–1741), and his last name was changed to Swedenborg (or Svedenborg). This change in status gave him a seat in the Swedish House of Nobles, where he remained an active participant in the Swedish government throughout his life.

A member of the Royal Swedish Academy of Sciences, he devoted himself to scientific studies and philosophical reflections that culminated in a number of publications, most notably a comprehensive three-volume work on mineralogy (1734) that brought him recognition across Europe as a scientist and philosopher. After 1734 he redirected his research and publishing to a study of anatomy in search of the interface between the soul and body, making several significant discoveries in physiology.

From 1743 to 1745 he entered a transitional phase that resulted in a shift of his main focus from science and philosophy to theology. Throughout the rest of his life he maintained that this shift was brought about by Jesus Christ, who appeared to him, called him to a new mission, and opened his perception to a permanent dual consciousness of this life and the life after death.

He devoted the last decades of his life to studying Scripture and publishing eighteen theological titles that draw on the Bible, reasoning, and his own spiritual experiences. These works present a Christian theology with unique perspectives on the nature of God, the spiritual world, the Bible, the human mind, and the path to salvation.

Swedenborg died in London on March 29, 1772, at the age of eighty-four.